THE TRAGEDY OF MANNERS

Moral Drama in the Later Novels of Henry James

THE TRAGEDY

OF MANNERS

Moral Drama in the Later Novels of Henry James

FREDERICK C. CREWS

ARCHON BOOKS, 1971

©1957 by Yale University Press, Inc.
Reprinted 1971 by Archon Books, an imprint of
The Shoe String Press, Inc., Hamden, Connecticut,
in an unaltered and unabridged edition with
permission. Printed in the United States of
America.
ISBN 0-208-01047-5
Library of Congress catalog card number: 77-131376

TO MY PARENTS

How can we know the dancer from the dance?

YEATS

PREFACE

THE SIZE AND WEIGHT of this volume should be testimony enough that it is not intended as a thorough study of James, or even of his later novels. My aim has been to present a running explication of *The Ambassadors*, *The Wings of the Dove*, and *The Golden Bowl* along what I consider to be the main outlines of those books—namely the dramatic opposition of certain moral and social values. In each case I have tried to show that all the action in a "Jamesian novel" may be taken as a result of philosophical differences of opinion among the principal characters, and that these differences in turn are explainable by reference to the characters' differing social backgrounds. James constantly shifts his emphasis from the social to the moral, and back again; we cannot deal with him simply in terms of one vocabulary or the other. Therefore I have endeavored in the first chapter to develop a method of analysis that can include both concepts, by showing how and why they become interchangeable in books like *The Portrait of a Lady* and *The Princess Casamassima*.

Any systematic method is bound to be more rigid than the literary work it is supposed to illuminate, and James's novels in particular have a subtlety and flexibility that criticism cannot reproduce. Indeed, the surfaces of his later novels are so ornate that James has been accused of lacking an underlying integrity of purpose; the opinion is still current that he became lost in the maze of his own style. My view is rather that the later complications of style are accompanied by a renewed, refined interest in structure. The later novels require not a separate method of analysis but a closer application of the method that best explains the action of the earlier works. The same values are at stake as before, and the same types of dramatic conflict derive from them.

The essential difference between the early and later James, then, does not lie in a gradual subversion of his moral sense. Where does the difference lie? Any answer in a study of such limited scope is bound to be incomplete, but I have addressed this question in a general way at the start of Chapter 2, and more specifically in treating each of the late novels. James's experimentation with form and theme is continued throughout the later period, and a definite pattern of development emerges when we consider the novels chronologically. One result of the development is that James's characters become less susceptible to moral categorization: it is increasingly difficult to divide the cast into heroes and villains. Near the end of *The Golden Bowl* the entire moral order implicit in the previous novels seems to come to a halt, and there is a new dispensation of mercy, a New Law if you like. At this point James himself apparently ceases to be a moral critic of his characters. However, I have argued at some length that this impression is only superficially true. Maggie Verver's mercy to her sinning husband is effected by a deliberate ambiguity of social manner on her part, but also by an aesthetic ambiguity of James's. In both cases the sacrifice consists merely in not saying what everyone already knows, and this seems faintly absurd until we realize how great is the temptation to return to the Old Law of severe justice and direct self-expression. The temptation is recorded only through innuendo, but it makes for the tremendous feeling of pressure that Maggie succeeds at last in over-coming. Her charity is meaningful only if we see that James's consciousness of evil is as strong as ever at the end. The triumph of aesthetic ambiguity, far from signaling an abandonment of morality, introduces a new and better morality, grounded on the old one but surmounting it. I have tried to show that throughout the later period James was probing in this direction, not only as a stylist but as a moral philosopher whose ideas were modified by the situations of his own fictional characters.

I wish to express my sincere thanks to the Hadley Fund and its administrators. Dean William C. DeVane has been especially helpful and kind to me. Happily, my greatest academic debts are owed to two of my favorite teachers. Martin Price is responsible for my interest in James in the first place, as well as for suggesting the general topic of this study. His advice and encouragement have been invaluable. Charles N. Feidelson, Jr., my adviser for the Senior Essay, has made available to me an understanding of James far deeper than my own, and has rescued me from many an error without once insisting on his own opinion. Professors Feidelson and Price together have aided me in the final revision of the essay for publication. I cannot express my full appreciation for the interest and integrity they have shown at every point. Among the other people at Yale who have encouraged me I might single out Davis Harding, who persuaded me to submit the essay for publication, and whose friendship has been constantly helpful. Finally, thanks are due the inevitable, indispensable typist—in this case my tireless mother.

Frederick C. Crews
Princeton, New Jersey

CONTENTS

CHAPTER 1

Society and the Hero

1.

ONE-THIRD of the way through James's *The Portrait of a Lady*, Isabel Archer, the heroine, discusses a problem of ethics with her new friend, Madame Merle. The immediate question is whether one should marry for money—an idea which Isabel finds unthinkable, but which Madame Merle, recalling her own sad experience, refuses to undervalue. When Isabel denies that she would care about the kind of house her supposed husband might own, Madame Merle replies frankly:

"That's very crude of you. When you've lived as long as I you'll see that every human being has his shell and that you must take the shell into account. By the shell I mean the whole envelope of circumstances. There's no such thing as an isolated man or woman; we're each of us made up of some cluster of appurtenances. What shall we call our 'self'? Where does it begin? where does it end? It overflows into everything that belongs to us—and then it flows back again. I know a large part of myself is in the clothes I choose to wear. I've a great respect for *things*! One's self—for other people— is one's expression of one's self; and one's house, one's furniture, one's garments, the books one reads, the company one keeps—these things are all expressive."

This was very metaphysical; not more so, however, than several observations Madame Merle had already made. Isabel was fond of metaphysics, but was unable to accompany her friend into this bold analysis of the human personality. "I don't agree with you. I think just the other way. I don't know whether I succeed in expressing myself, but I know that nothing else expresses me. Nothing that belongs to me is any measure of me; everything's on the contrary a limit, a barrier, and a perfectly arbitrary one. Certainly the clothes which, as you say, I choose to wear, don't express me; and heaven forbid they should!"

"You dress very well," Madame Merle lightly interposed.

"Possibly; but I don't care to be judged by that. My clothes may express the dressmaker, but they don't express me. To begin with it's not my own choice that I wear them; they're imposed upon me by society."

"Should you prefer to go without them?" Madame Merle enquired in a tone which virtually terminated the discussion.[1]

The two attitudes that are outlined in this condensed form deserve close attention, for they establish what amounts to a metaphysical basis for Madame Merle's and Isabel's differing attitudes toward marriage. This in turn is the key to most of the novel's action. The principal subject of our attention in the first half of the book is the wooing of Isabel by various suitors of different qualifications, so that the question of whether she will make a marriage of convenience is uppermost in our minds. In the second half of the book the same question is posed for her stepdaughter, Pansy. Madame Merle deliberately matches Isabel with her own ex-lover, Gilbert Osmond, whom she herself never married precisely because he had no money. This apparent digression about one's "envelope of circumstances," introduced as it is by the question of marrying for practical advantage, is thus in retrospect the most portentous argument in the novel.

The point of difference between Madame Merle and Isabel is a matter of definition: "What shall we call our 'self'?" Isabel feels it wrong to consider one's real self as overlapping with the more or less accidental circumstances of one's fortune. She sees the individual soul as completely independent of "society": if one's self is indefinable, it is nonetheless real and autonomous. It is "limited"—that is, obscured from view—by society's "perfectly arbitrary" impositions, but it is not limited in the other meaning of that word. Society does not prescribe its borders. For Madame Merle, on the contrary, the outer limits of one's self are determined by the context in which it exists. Furthermore, she sees that context as "expressive" of one's inner qualities, not only because one has a certain measure of freedom in choosing where and how he will live, but because these circumstances *interact* with the self. Whereas Isabel thinks of the soul as a fixed entity, sacred and unalterable, Madame Merle sees it as pliable, subject to enrichment or impoverishment by favorable or unfavorable opportunities. She therefore considers it a matter of spiritual as well as practical importance that Isabel make a congenial marriage, i.e. one that will provide a

1. Henry James, *The Portrait of a Lady* (London, Oxford University Press, 1954), p. 216. Courtesy of Paul R. Reynolds & Son, 599 Fifth Avenue, New York.

healthy share of beneficial "things." Isabel, on the contrary, sees this attitude as a grievous confusion of the material and the spiritual.

It is worth noting that although this argument is, as Isabel thinks, "very metaphysical," the two contrasting positions do not reflect a fundamental disagreement about the nature of reality. The key sentence is Madame Merle's "One's self—*for other people*—is one's expression of one's self." The difference is literally one of point of view. Madame Merle sees herself as others see her, from the outside, while Isabel sees herself from the inside only. Madame Merle, as we finally learn from a statement she makes to Osmond about his influence on her, believes in the soul's existence and importance just as much as Isabel does. She simply prefers to define it in terms of the external circumstances that surround it, and which present "other people" with its only visible manifestation. Isabel's interest does not lie in the visible; if no one can perceive the true essence of her being, so much the better for its sanctity. Other people may possibly mistake the shell for the core, but she herself will dismiss all external evidence, not only in her own case but in judging others as well.

From the fact that Madame Merle is a villain and Isabel a heroine in the subsequent action it is tempting to conclude that Isabel's point of view must be the proper one. However, a careful reading of the novel calls this into question. Madame Merle's own career seems to support her side of the argument. Like Isabel, she refused to take external advantages into account when she married, and as a result her subsequent life, moral as well as material, has been ruined. We cannot tell how much her soul has been altered, but by her own admission there is very little remaining. When Osmond hypocritically describes the soul as an immutable, immortal principle, Madame Merle's answer has a ring of truth: "I don't believe at all that it's an immortal principle. I believe it can perfectly be destroyed. That's what has happened to mine, which was a very good one to start with . . ." (p. 569) What is more, Isabel herself is gradually brought around to a partial acceptance of this attitude. Her own marriage to a man whose exterior is false has an adverse effect not only on the freedom of her manners, but on her very capacity for living. At the end, it is true, she faces her ordeal with some degree of hope that she may emerge from it whole, but we have already witnessed the beginnings of her petrifaction. And when her stepdaughter Pansy becomes involved in a situation much the same as her own—a choice of blindly following her heart's inclination or deliberately "marrying well"—Isabel significantly leans toward recommending the latter alternative. She remains convinced that money is of secondary importance, but she has learned Madame Merle's lesson that the heart cannot be trusted as the sole judge of its own welfare. As for the ultimate question of whether one's self really "overflows into everything that belongs to us," this is left unresolved. It is certain only that one's self can be *influenced,* for better or worse, by practical circumstances.

The point I want especially to emphasize is that this difference in philosophy not only is central to a consideration of final meaning in *The Portrait of a Lady* but is a means of precipitating the action of the book in the first place. Everything that happens may be taken as a gloss on the little debate about metaphysics, for each of the characters implicitly defends one side or the other, and is socially aided or handicapped by his position. With differing points of view the characters will see different sides of the truth, and consequently they will react differently to a given situation. Thus Henrietta Stackpole and Caspar Goodwood, Isabel's American friends, are incapable of dealing successfully with Osmond and Madame Merle because they know nothing about the meaning of "appearances." Ralph Touchett, whom Isabel finally recognizes as her spiritual brother, cannot convince her that her engagement to Osmond is imprudent. When he says that he had believed she would marry someone "of more importance," she explodes, "Of more importance to whom? It seems to be enough that one's husband should be of importance to one's self!" (p. 372) As she proudly tells Caspar Goodwood, "I don't marry for my friends." (p. 355) This may show an admirable independence, but it prevents her from escaping from a situation in which her independence will perish. Not believing that anyone can understand her invisible "real self," she renders herself impervious to the advice that might have saved her.

But the philosophical basis of her mistake lies even deeper than this. She marries Osmond not in disregard of Madame Merle's position, but in a conscious defiance of it. She has inherited a large sum of money unexpectedly, and she must prove to herself that it makes no difference to her. "What would lighten her own conscience more effectually than to make it over to the man with the best taste in the world?" (p. 464) While Osmond is secretly desperate for money, Isabel is anxious to get rid of it, and she is drawn to him precisely because she can spend it on the distinctions he seems to appreciate aesthetically. "It's the total absence of all these things that pleases me" (p. 376), she explains to Ralph. But after the marriage she sees that Osmond, even more than Madame Merle, identifies his real self with his social pose. He despises what he can only regard as false righteousness in Isabel—since he too is limited in vision by his definition of the self—and cannot believe that she is sincere in placing her "unsocial" affection for Pansy and Ralph above his own narrow sense of propriety. As for Madame Merle, whose elaborate deceptions have been motivated largely by a desire to secure the happiness of Pansy, her daughter by Osmond, she too is victimized by the difference between an "internal" and "external" view of reality. Pansy distrusts and dislikes her, and Isabel, whose life she has effectively ruined, banishes her from Pansy's company. At the end each character has been sorely disappointed, and for the same reason: each has taken it for granted that the philosophies of the others were sufficiently close to his own.

In the present study I am concerned primarily not with *The Portrait of a Lady*, but with James's three great novels of twenty years later: *The Ambassadors, The Wings of the Dove,* and *The Golden Bowl*. I have begun with this glimpse of *The Portrait* because that novel seems to me to state with remarkable clarity a situation and a problem that we shall be dealing with later in a more complicated form. The situation—which I shall illustrate at greater length with reference to another early novel, *The Princess Casamassima*—is that of the naïve but morally scrupulous hero in the presence of a world more sophisticated than his own. The problem is that of moral responsibility. In *The Portrait of a Lady* we are confronted with two villains and a heroine whose dramatic opposition may seem at first to call for a simple moral condemnation of the former and endorsement of the latter, but who gradually lead us away from such a judgment. Certainly Isabel's actions are more praiseworthy than Osmond's or Madame Merle's; there is no question about the identity of the "Lady" in the title. But Isabel, the unimpeachable heroine, moves reluctantly toward an acceptance of the very attitude of her enemies, or at least to a significant part of that attitude. Although her moral stature is greater than ever at the end of the novel, she has cast doubt on her original philosophy of the soul's invulnerability; indeed, her vulnerability is the source of our final uneasiness about her future. The basis for a flat condemnation of Osmond and Madame Merle has thus been somewhat weakened, for it appears that their attitude was at least partially justified by the course of events. To be sure, we have very little sympathy for them, and especially for Osmond. But how can we say they are damned? James has provided us with a more or less plausible explanation for their attitude on philosophical grounds, and if we accept their philosophy we cannot dismiss their application of it. This philosophy has been gleaned from bitter experience; it is the fruit of their moral environment. Perhaps, then, we should ask whether such characters are truly responsible, as individuals, for their own moral principles. Is there such a thing as free will? Are we justified in speaking of "villains" at all in James's novels? I do not pretend to have simple answers to these questions, but I do feel—as several prominent critics do not—that exactly the same problem is at issue in the later novels. Why are certain actions made necessary, and who if anyone is truly responsible for them?

In still broader terms the question may be stated as the characters' relationship to society. What constitutes "society," and how should the fictional hero react to it? The quoted argument between Isabel Archer and Madame Merle juxtaposes two opposite attitudes toward society. For Isabel, society is an external force that has nothing basically to do with her dignity as an individual. At the end of the novel she has come to see it as a threat to that dignity, but by no means as a component of it. Madame Merle sees dignity itself as a social concept. Honesty, decency, tact—these virtues are all dependent on a congenial atmosphere. To be deprived of social advantages is to be deprived of dignity itself. The action of the novel, as I pointed out, has a continual relevance to this disagreement. To this extent I should say that we are justified in calling it "moral" action. The development and resolution of the main crisis, when read on the highest level that James seems to expect, are symbolic of the latent implications in contrasting an "internal" with an "external" attitude toward one's self and others. Isabel's whole adventure may be called a lesson in the redefinition of her self.

The Jamesian hero as we shall meet him in the later novels repeats this development, but on a more comprehensive scale. We see Isabel before and after her reappraisal of values, but not during the most crucial period, the first years of her marriage. In the later novels, and particularly in *The Ambassadors,* this process of education takes place before our eyes—and yet with a degree of understatement and obscurity which may prevent us from grasping the simplest facts. To meet this danger I want to outline the basic pattern of the hero's education as it occurs in *The Princess Casamassima* before going on to speak of *The Ambassadors*. Although the earlier book is less challenging from a technical point of view, its action is based on the same kind of moral contrast, and its hero is subjected to a similar social ordeal. He enters society as a relative stranger, weighs its values against his own, and gradually extends his moral consciousness until he can see his life in an ultimate, nonsocial perspective. From this point of vision, which is undoubtedly closest to the author's, all the previous action of the novel is implicitly judged.

2.

The Princess Casamassima, written in 1885–86, is the most clearly "social" of all James's works. It deals with society not only as a developing concept in the hero's mind, but as a literal struggle of the classes as well. The ostensible subject is a revolutionary movement in London, and Lionel Trilling and others, including James himself, have argued that the feeling of deep social unrest in the 1880's was the literal inspiration for the book. If so, the inspiration was not very compelling, for, as Daniel Lerner has shown, before James finished he had resorted to Turgenev's *Virgin Soil* for the bulk of his plot and characters.[2] However, we need not regret this fact. James reminded himself in his preliminary notes that "The subject of the *Princess* is magnificent,"[3] and in his own manner of writing he did it full justice. What he borrowed from Turgenev's book was a concern for the mind of a single hero who is trapped between a desire for social revolution and a growing respect for the doomed aristocracy. The revolution has not occurred at the end, and we see virtually none of its preparation. Whether or not James was capable of describing the omitted scenes, it is certain that as the novel progressed he chose his material solely with the expanding consciousness of his hero in mind. The result is quite the opposite of a book about open revolution. It is a book about reflection and reconsideration.

Hyacinth Robinson is a young man whose natural sensitivity has been sharpened by a basic insecurity in his circumstances. His parentage is partly uncertain, involving a French prostitute and possibly a dis-

2. Daniel Lerner, "The Influence of Turgenev on Henry James," *Slavonic and East European Review, 20* (1941), 28–54.

3. *The Notebooks of Henry James,* eds. F. O. Matthiessen and Kenneth B. Murdock (New York, George Braziller, Inc., 1955), p. 68.

solute English nobleman. He is adopted by an undistinguished London seamstress, and appears destined to be raised as a laborer of her class. But his ambiguous background haunts him. The seamstress is herself obsessed with the idea that he may have noble blood, and Hyacinth comes to share this pretension. He sees himself as a disinherited aristocrat, caught between the upper and lower classes—his "natural" and his actual homes, respectively. Psychologically speaking, these two forces converge on the hero and eventually cause his death. As Hyacinth becomes increasingly aware of the irreconcilability of his two ideals— justice for the lower classes and "culture" for the upper—he steadily revises his opinion of both groups, and emerges from the conflict (albeit as a corpse) with a moral transcendence of them both.

James deliberately confuses the issue of whether Hyacinth's gentle manners are due literally to his parentage or to his developing conception of himself as an aristocrat. The confusion is valuable artistically, not only because Hyacinth himself is unable to separate fact from legend in his background, but because this background has a symbolic relevance to the whole course of the plot. His mother, who murdered his supposed father, represents "the people" for him, and his father becomes an image of the aristocracy. The murder itself prefigures the clash and eventual explosion of mother-forces and father-forces in the hero's mind, and also suggests the literal war of classes promised by the leaders of the revolution.

Hyacinth is in a sense victimized by the legendary flavor of his situation. Instead of taking positive action along one possible line or another, he allows himself to become obsessed, like Hamlet, with the moral complications of his dilemma. When he has reached the stage where he is taking the social "influence" of his parents on an entirely literal level, this moral scrupulousness threatens to disrupt his mind:

There was no peace for him between the two currents that flowed in his nature, the blood of his passionate, plebeian mother and that of his long-descended, supercivilised sire. They continued to toss him from one side to the other; they arrayed him in intolerable defiances and revenges against himself. He had a high ambition: he wanted neither more nor less than to get hold of the truth and wear it in his heart. He believed with the candour of youth that it is brilliant and clear-cut, like a royal diamond; but to whatever quarter he turned in the effort to find it he seemed to know that behind him, bent on him in reproach, was a tragic, wounded face. The thought of his mother had filled him with the vague, clumsy fermentation of his first impulses toward social criticism; but since the problem had become more complex by the fact that many things in the world as it was constituted were to grow intensely dear to him he had tried more and more to construct some conceivable and human countenance for his father—some expression of honour, of tenderness and recognition, of unmerited suffering, or at least of adequate expiation.[4]

Hyacinth feels that in order to "get hold of the truth and wear it in his heart" he must first exorcise the image of a criminal father. Ironically enough, this very effort will lead him to the truth, in social terms. The attempt to "construct some conceivable and human countenance" for a member of a class with which he is totally unfamiliar will drive Hyacinth to a sympathy with the best ideals of English nobility, and when this attitude is joined with the lower-class virtues he began with, he will have arrived at a nonsocial, superior "truth"; i.e. he will have escaped from the constrictions and prejudices of any single pattern of training. In speaking of his motivation we can use as a starting point either this psychological compulsion of parent-seeking, or the literal and figurative division of influence in his birth, or simply his desire for a comprehensive ideal of human dignity; James carefully preserves the validity of all three possibilities. But in any case we must accept Hyacinth's word that his social adventures are dictated by a genuine concern for truth, a passion for reality. "It was not so much that he wanted to enjoy as that he wanted to know." (*1*, 150) From the point of view of the novel's structure, the cause of his eventual death may be said to be an overdose of truth.

The vision Hyacinth acquires combines the best insights of Isabel Archer and Madame Merle in the passage quoted from *The Portrait of a Lady*. He begins his career with a conviction of his intrinsic nobility of spirit—a faith that is entirely justified, but which is based on a scanty awareness of the rest of the world. What he acquires is a sense of proportion and limitation, a knowledge that the soul's natural dignity can be nourished or stunted by external circumstances. If we follow the growth of Hyacinth's moral consciousness, we can see that it is exactly parallel to the gradual refinement of his attitude toward society. Indeed, they are two sides of the same coin. To define one's relation to society is to make visible the outer borders of one's self, and conscience appears to derive from this very sense of the self as finite and hence responsible to its neighbors.

Hyacinth's affiliation with the working class of London allows him

4. *The Princess Casamassima* (2 vols. New York, Macmillan, 1948), *2*, 237.

to defer his serious interest in the aristocracy until he is a young man in his twenties. Inspired by the thought of the wrong that society has done to his mother, whom he has been taken to visit on her prison deathbed, he concerns himself at first only with the question of social justice. But his innate sensitivity and his growing acquaintance with the "things" for which Madame Merle showed such respect begin to complicate this attitude. He chooses the vocation of bookbinder, embracing both art and manual labor. This is an early effort to adjust the claims of his two social affinities. However, it also amounts to the first step toward an aesthetically grounded disgust with the lower classes.

It was both a blessing and a drawback to him that the delicate, charming character of the work he did at Old Crook's, under Eustache Poupin's influence, was a kind of education of the taste, trained him in the finest discriminations, in the recognition of the rare and the hatred of the cheap. This made the brutal, garish, stodgy decoration of public-houses, with their deluge of gaslight, their glittering brass and pewter, their lumpish woodwork and false colours, detestable to him. He had been still very young when the "gin-palace" ceased to convey to him an idea of the palatial. [*1*, 141]

At this point Hyacinth's interest is divided between two men, Eustache Poupin and Paul Muniment. The contradiction in the French side of his nature is implicitly stated in his friendship with Poupin. Like Hyacinth's mother, Poupin is "of the people"; indeed, he is a member of the revolutionary movement. Being French involves a certain pretense to elegance, however, and this is satirically contrasted with his anarchism. Hyacinth secretly delights in his own Frenchness. His craftsmanship shows "*la main parisienne*" (*1*, 98), and he takes pride in his French gestures and his command of the language. When he finally visits Paris he feels it to be his "ancestral city." (*2*, 111) But Paris, like Eustache Poupin, implies a twin ideal: on the one hand, individual cultivation, but on the other, revolution and equality. Although Hyacinth still believes that both are possible, he finds himself increasingly reminded that his own case is an especially difficult one. His pretensions to nobility of blood are also his ties to a dissolute, immoral man, and his pretensions to French elegance involve him with a prostitute-murderess. As James puts it wryly, "the reflexion that he was a bastard involved in a remarkable manner the reflexion that he was a gentleman." (*1*, 154f.) This paradox keeps Hyacinth from seeing himself with any of the biases of one class or another.

His friendship with Paul Muniment carries with it his hope that "the people" (he later questions the validity of the term) represent a worthy object for his revolutionary zeal. Paul has none of the brash reckless-ness of his fellow radicals. He is strong, calm, and sincerely dedicated to the cause of reform, even after he has fallen in love with a member of the aristocracy. However, he finally fails in Hyacinth's eyes, not because he betrays the revolution, but on the contrary because he shows himself exclusively faithful to it. His political discretion keeps him aloof from all display of human feeling. When Hyacinth meets this coldness as he is preparing to sacrifice his life for the revolution, he realizes that he has deluded himself not only about Paul's humanity but about the moral value of anarchism as well.

Although Paul and the revolution are now equally unattractive, it is still possible that Hyacinth may retain a faith in "the people"; Paul is a leader, not an average representative of the masses. *The Princess* does provide us with such a figure in the person of Millicent Henning, per-haps the most delightfully "average" member of her group—the lower middle class—that James created. She is energetic, superstitious, vulgar, naïve, coquettish, healthy, and above all, ambitious. Hyacinth sees in her everything that attracts and repels him in the common herd:

Millicent, to hear her talk, only asked to keep her skirts clear and marry some respectable tea-merchant. But for our hero she was magnificently plebeian, in the sense that implied loud recklessness of danger and the qualities that shine forth in a row. She summed up the sociable humorous ignorant chatter of the masses, their capacity for offensive and defensive passion, their instinctive per-ception of their strength on the day they should really exercise it; and as much as any of this their ideal of something smug and prosperous, where washed hands and oiled hair and plates in rows on dressers and stuffed birds under glass and family photographs of a quite similar effect would symbolise success. She was none the less plucky for being at bottom a shameless Philistine, ambitious of a front garden with rockwork; and she presented the plebeian character in none the less plastic a form. [*1*, 145f.]

Millicent has no taste for revolutions, but she is full of the energy and courage of the ambitious working class. At one point, indeed, James likens her to "Liberty Leading the People." (*1*, 146) It is wrong to think that Hyacinth's awareness of her crudity makes her any the less attractive to him. In Millicent he finds a clumsy but genuine maternal quality that the Princess Casamassima lacks, and which makes him feel for a while that Millicent's class, for all its limitations of taste, is his genuine home. It is important to our weighing of the social question in this book to remember that after the Princess has discarded him Hyacinth returns to Millicent for comfort.

As long as Hyacinth is content to bind books rather than compose them, and while he still endorses the political ideals of his lower-class friends, his latent conflict is not brought to the surface. The theory that the wealthy should enjoy their wealth is held only by Rosy Muniment, whom Hyacinth secretly dislikes, and the only aristocrat in the early chapters, Lady Aurora Langrish, is ashamed that she can't give all her possessions to the poor. But by the time the Princess Casamassima is introduced, Hyacinth's love of fine objects has carried him on its own strength a long way toward the aristocratic ideal. In moods of depression "he felt how in this world of effort and suffering life was endurable, the spirit able to expand, only in the best conditions, and how a sordid struggle in which one should go down to the grave without having tasted them was not worth the misery it would cost, the dull demoralisation it would involve." (*1*, 149) Hyacinth has begun to see that the ideal of complete equality is in practice an ideal of mediocrity, and he now fears mediocrity more than inequality. Furthermore, he recognizes and repents of an element of unjustifiable envy in his righteous contempt for the rich. "I don't know what it comes from, but during the last three months there has crept over me a deep mistrust of that same grudging attitude—the intolerance of positions and fortunes that are higher and brighter than one's own; a fear, moreover, that I may in the past have been actuated by such motives, and a devout hope that if I'm to pass away while I'm yet young it may not be with that odious stain upon my soul." (*2*, 130f.) Critics who feel that Hyacinth's interest in the aristocracy is a lapse of conscience, a simple indulgence of the senses, might do well to bear this religious vocabulary in mind.

Just before meeting the Princess Casamassima, Hyacinth has decided that he must choose between his two ideals; he must "either suffer with the people as he had suffered before, or he must apologise . . . for the rich." (*1*, 151) The Princess defers this choice, for she successfully presents to him an image of personal cultivation joined with democratic fervor. At the same time that her subtlety, her gracefulness, and her *objets d'art* surround her with an air of complete freedom, her sponsorship of the revolution places her, for Hyacinth, on the highest moral plane. Altogether she seems to be "the most remarkable woman in Europe." The course of the book is now divided into two streams, the Princess' increasing involvement with the revolution and Hyacinth's increasing disappointment with it. He falls in love with her, and sees the accomplishments of her mind—including her ability to be so disinterested that she can plot the downfall of her fellow aristocrats—as evidence that the aristocracy is worth preserving. The latent irony in this situation is pointed with more and more force as Hyacinth and the Princess, under the influence of each other's example, move toward a renunciation of their respective classes. Because the Princess "believes in" Hyacinth and his comrades she is willing to betray the aristocracy, and Hyacinth comes to feel that a revolution cannot be morally sound which will destroy such magnanimity as the Princess'.

Hyacinth's developing social consciousness enables him to see, finally, that the upper classes have a special vulgarity of their own. The Princess' friends are dull and narrow. But this only makes the Princess herself seem all the more admirable. Hyacinth regards her as utterly beyond the prejudices of her class, and attributes this achievement to her proper use of the opportunities afforded by an aristocratic marriage. He considers the ease with which she can be bored not as a characteristic of her social group but as the sign of a delicate, discriminating taste. She calls herself classless, and Hyacinth believes her. However, the reader sees what Hyacinth, through a lack of acquaintance with princesses, cannot possibly see: her behavior is no less socially conditioned than Millicent Henning's. Her class is one degree above the rich and one degree below reigning royalty; in short, just the stage at which freedom is divorced from responsibility. She was not born into this class, she schemed her way into it; and having climbed as high as she can possibly go, she has found herself disillusioned with the fruits of her ambition and completely alone with her conscience. Everything she does is now a search to find some object on which to lavish her energy and talent—or, in social terms, to revitalize herself from below. As Lionel Trilling says in his penetrating introduction to the book, she is "a perfect drunkard of reality." (*1,* xlvi) Her interest in Hyacinth and the revolution is traceable in large measure to this passion, half-frivolous and half-earnest. It is, as she puts it herself, a need to substitute the *naïf* for the *banal.* "To do something for others was not only so much more human—it was so much more amusing!" (*2,* 234)

The Princess' confidante, Madame Grandoni, is by contrast thoroughly proud of her membership in the aristocracy, and has no illusions about the "idealistic" motivation of the Princess' interest in revolt. Her respect for class distinctions is based not on snobbery but on a feeling that no one can find fulfillment outside of the social world that has educated him. Thus she sees Hyacinth as morally endangered by his attraction to the Princess, and she pleads with him not to "give himself up." But Hyacinth fails to see what she means. In the act of binding a book for the Princess he symbolically puts himself in her hands. He endows the book with an aura that he assumes to be the Princess', "as if a ghost in vanishing from sight had left a palpable relic." (1, 265) The "ghost in vanishing" is an aristocracy once creative but now sterile and decadent, unable to know the value of its own inherited treasures. That Hyacinth, the real aristocrat in sensibility, should be "condemned to see these things only from outside—in mere quickened consideration, mere wistfulness and envy and despair"[5] is a modern irony indeed. The injustice is capped when we later learn that the Princess herself has no sense of Hyacinth's importance as a maker of noble objects. She accepts his books with the same self-righteous boredom she shows to everyone who is, in her opinion, promoting invidious social distinctions. In denying the value of Hyacinth's craftsmanship she is not simply undermining his only healthy attachment to a social reality, she is giving the lie to her own pretense of true nobility. An aristocracy without a respect for aesthetic values is a class divorced from its one excuse for existence. It is a very grim joke on James's part that the Princess "considered that she too was one of the numerous class who could be put on a tolerable footing only by a revolution." (1, 259)

Just as Hyacinth is about to lose his heart to the Princess and her world, he takes an oath to risk his life for the cause of anarchism. He feels all the poignancy of his situation when he is now exposed to the splendor of the Princess' country estate. As James mentions in his preface, "The complication most interesting then would be that he should fall in love with the beauty of the world, actual order and all, at the moment of his most feeling and most hating the famous 'iniquity of its social arrangements'; so that his position as an irreconcileable pledged enemy to it, thus rendered false by something more personal than his opinions and his vows, becomes the sharpest of his torments."[6] When he returns to London to find that his foster mother has been

5. Henry James, *The Art of the Novel*, ed. Richard P. Blackmur (New York and London, Scribner's, 1934), p. 60.
6. *Ibid.*, p. 72.

dying in his absence, all his remorse cannot prevent him from recognizing that his old home sickens him. He now sees that in spirit he is utterly dedicated to the world that the Princess wants destroyed in the name of social justice. Only his oath of honor—an oath that Hyacinth takes seriously precisely because he *is* a genuine aristocrat—now binds him to the revolution. Occasionally, it is true, he sees a ghastly aesthetic harmony in the sweep of the movement—a "great symphonic massacre"—but his own part in it will be paltry and humiliating: "The day would come when—far down in the treble—one would feel one's self touched by the little finger of the composer, would grow generally audible (with a small sharp crack) for a second." (2, 50) Only in a climate of art can Hyacinth find the proper expression of his dignity, and the revolution's stand on the subject of art is neatly captured in Hyacinth's speculation about what the leader, Deidrich Hoffendahl, would do if he came to power: "He would cut up the ceilings of the Veronese into strips, so that every one might have a little piece." (2, 130)

Hyacinth's self-cultivation eventually disqualifies him in the Princess' eyes as a member of the working class, and she therefore appears to lose interest in him; he is becoming too like herself. Significantly, her fascination with Paul Muniment dates from the hour when she learns that he has warned Hyacinth against her. She and Paul can benefit mutually from their acquaintance. Paul needs her money for the revolution, and it is hinted that he also loves her for her own sake. To the Princess, Paul represents the stark simplicity, the ambition, the innocence (although false innocence) of the rising masses. Unlike Hyacinth, Paul understands just what she expects from him, and he is willing to play the part. As he states it himself, he is her "chaplain." This clarity of mind in Paul eventually shows him something that does not occur in the book, but which we may expect to happen immediately after the Princess discovers Hyacinth's death. She will give up her radicalism. The revolution will take its place among the numerous objects and causes to which she has tried unsuccessfully to adhere, but her fundamental loyalty to Hyacinth will outlast them all. This is because in Hyacinth she must recognize the truest image of herself—lonely, large-souled, and essentially without a social home. Hyacinth is seeking to find his identity, but he will lose his life as a consequence. The Princess, on the other hand, has been trying to hide her identity in a kind of ultimate snobbery, a contempt for the distinction she has plotted to acquire. But in her reaction to Hyacinth's tragedy she will know that she has failed.

When the Princess deserts him Hyacinth turns back to Millicent, and for a while he obtains a certain consolation from her artless sensuousness. Millicent and only Millicent could say things like: "Well, there's nothing so pretty as nature." (2, 296) After the company of the blasé Princess this is a refreshing change. However, Hyacinth's thoughts are now dominated by the act of terrorism he has finally been asked to commit; there is no question of escape. In Millicent he only revives his hope that "the people" may be worth dying for after all. But when he is suddenly struck with evidence of her attachment to the vulgar adventurer, Captain Sholto, he sees an indelible image of the cheapness that the revolution proposes to make universal, and he kills himself instead of his assigned victim.

Although Hyacinth has been, as Paul accuses him, "a duke in disguise" (2, 193) all along, it should be emphasized that his final attitude is not a simple endorsement of the aristocracy. The knowledge of his impossible commitment has lifted him above the issue of choosing one class or another as his own. What he has achieved is a vision of human society as a whole, and his attitude toward it is that of an artist, not a member of a social group. James symbolizes the scope of this vision in Hyacinth's awareness of London when he returns from the Continent:

The influence of his permeating London had closed over him again; Paris and Milan and Venice had shimmered away into reminiscence and picture; and as the great city which was most his own lay round him under her pall like an immeasurable breathing monster he felt with a vague excitement, as he had felt before, only now with more knowledge, that it was the richest expression of the life of man. His horizon had been immensely widened, but it was filled again by the expanse that sent dim night-gleams and strange, blurred reflexions and emanations into a sky without stars. He suspended, so to say, his small sensibility in the midst of it, to quiver there with joy and hope and ambition as well as with the effort of renunciation. [2, 239]

This is what Keats called negative capability; not detachment from life, but a universal participation in it. Hyacinth's adventure in society has narrowed his sense of individual possibility at the same time that it has greatly expanded his definition of the outside world, his sense of all possibilities taken together. As a result he is more respectful of life in general—of "the life of man"—than any member of a social class could possibly be, for each class has its comfortable untruths about the size of the rest of the world. Whether he wants to be or not, Hyacinth is in the presence of truth itself, and his suicide is at once an affirmation of the existence of this truth and a despair of its congeniality to life. We can say, of course, that he is killed by his practical dilemma, or by his disillusionment with his friends; both of these motives should be considered first. But on a different level his death is made necessary by the philosophical structure of the novel. He must die because with his new vision there is no place left for him to live. This vision has been reached, and is expressed, in social terms. Social conflict not only determines the context and superficial plot of the novel, it gradually forces the hero into an attitude which enables him in effect to escape from society altogether. Yet the very act of escape, in this case, is an act of suicide. Therefore I call *The Princess Casamassima* a tragedy of manners.

CHAPTER 2

The Ambassadors

1.

IT IS A FACT perhaps too well known that James's later novels are not easy to read. If we approach them with anything less than the closest and most patient attention, or with an expectation of being entertained as Fielding and Dickens and Thackeray can entertain us, we shall neither understand nor enjoy them. There is little that is "lifelike" about them in the ordinary use of that term. The strategy of James's later style was not to represent but to disguise the "lifelike touches" which abound in his own early works. Critics who have disliked the ambiguities, hesitations, and lengthy periods of the later style have been inclined to set these things down to inadvertence, to a loss of the power to be concrete. However, James himself regarded them as deliberate and necessary elements in the total effect of his novels. Obscurity was not something to be avoided but rather to be cultivated, in order to secure the highest intensity of interest on the reader's part. The luxury of art is greatest, he wrote in his preface to *The Wings of the Dove,* "when we feel the surface, like the thick ice of the skater's pond, bear without cracking the strongest pressure we throw on it."[1] This is an ideal not of noncommunication, but rather of inviting as much communication as possible.

The depth of the later novels is achieved in part by a restriction of their width. They record no historical crises, show us a minimum of background scenery, and contain no philosophical reflections irrelevant to the scenes at hand. Instead, they begin with a basic practical situation and then explore every influence that the situation can have upon the few characters who are involved in it. The means to complexity lies in the characters themselves. They are enormously sensitive to moral and intellectual shades of meaning that would remain unper-

1. *The Art of the Novel,* pp. 304f.

ceived by ordinary people. In effect they are superhuman, larger than life, but they perceive nothing that is not latent in the situation before them. Given their exceptional capacity for reflection and analysis, we cannot say that they misrepresent the truth of their experience, for that experience is conditioned by their very receptivity.[2] Although they concentrate only on their relations with each other, they bring such extraordinary sensitiveness to bear on those relations that the simplest facts become charged with significance.

James's technical ideal in these books was to eliminate every extraneous factor from the situation at hand. Hazard, whim, coincidence— these were tricks of plotting to which the novelist should not resort. As he wrote in "The Art of Fiction," "What is character but the determination of incident? What is incident but the illustration of character?"[3] It is possible to see most of the differences between the earlier and later novels as deriving from the serious application of this concept in the later works. With a very few exceptions there are no unexpected, externally caused events to complicate or change the characters' attitudes.[4] Rather, each event results from an improvement in comprehension of events that have gone before. The question is not, as in most novels, "What is going to happen next?" but rather "What is the meaning of that which has already happened?" At any given

2. James's idea of the subjective nature of truth in human perception may be suggested by this passage from "The Art of Fiction": "Experience is never limited, and it is never complete; it is an immense sensibility, a kind of huge spider-web of the finest silken threads suspended in the chamber of consciousness, and catching every air-borne particle in its tissue. It is the very atmosphere of the mind; and when the mind is imaginative . . . it [the mind] takes to itself the faintest hints of life, it converts the very pulses of the air into revelations." (Reprinted in *Criticism: the Foundations of Modern Literary Judgment,* eds. Mark Schorer et al. New York, Harcourt, Brace, 1948, p. 48.) Experience is not an external chain of events but "an immense sensibility"; it is inseparable from the texture of one's mind. If the mind is extremely receptive, it will find truth in impressions that other minds do not receive at all. Thus for James there is no such thing as a restricted body of experiences that are "true to life."

3. "The Art of Fiction," p. 50.

4. When coincidences do occur, they have been elaborately prepared for on a symbolic level, so that they appear to be determined by the natural development of the situation. For example, Maggie Verver's finding of the same cracked golden bowl that was almost given her as a wedding present by her adulterous husband and his mistress signifies her final awareness of the adultery. In *The Ambassadors,* Strether's unexpected meeting of Chad and Madame de Vionnet in the country has the same force. "What he saw was exactly the right thing . . . It was suddenly as if these figures, or something like them, had been wanted in the picture, had been wanted, more or less, all day, and had now drifted into sight, with the slow current, on purpose to fill up the measure." *The Ambassadors* (New York, Harper, 1948), p. 382.

point James professes to know only as much as his characters do. The reader and the characters together are coaxed into ever larger realizations, yet always with the sense of their perceptual limits before them. We are forever on the verge of solving a crucial mystery, or rather by solving it we enable ourselves to see further mysteries behind it. Like Proust and Kafka, James thus presents us with a world in which reality is kept just around the corner. His characters, by being remarkably perceptive and yet finding themselves still ignorant of the most important facts, illustrate his belief that no single awareness of life is adequate in itself. The elaborate, groping, often ambiguous sentences in which these novels are written serve this feeling directly. Completely aside from action, method alone becomes an instrument of meaning.

James's concern for strength of surface is shared by his characters, who insist on preserving their good manners at all times. Each of the major figures feels obliged to be polite to the others, even when it means suppressing the most urgent feelings. In effect this is a method of complicating and intensifying the drama, for it makes it difficult for each character (and for the reader) to tell what the others are thinking. It is common practice for resolute enemies to take considerable pains for each other's comfort and to express the tenderest mutual sentiments. Only in the slightest gestures, the barest inconsistencies of politeness is the real emotional drama beneath the surface perceived. The language of good manners thus provides a kind of circumlocution for the action it hides, and when simple facts do finally emerge, they seem all the more stark by contrast with the pervading atmosphere of courtesy. But since James does not contradict his characters when they use their good manners hypocritically, it is hard to decide who is sincere and who isn't. However, it is significant that the basic moral contrasts of the early novels are repeated in the later ones; if we are sufficiently familiar with the moral issue we can follow the logic of the action.

What is it that James's true heroes have in common? We saw at the end of *The Princess Casamassima* that Hyacinth Robinson had achieved a moral superiority to every influence in his past life. He became a moral hero not by rejecting his previous imperfect ideals but by acknowledging their destructive grasp on him. He ended in a selfless passion for knowledge, an awareness of life-as-a-whole (designated below as "Life") rather than an endorsement of one way of living against another. We shall see this pattern repeated in the later novels.

The true hero has an aesthetic sense of Life's vastness and diversity, and he prizes this vision above every other goal. He will do anything to preserve it. In practice this means that he will look for a measure of validity in every attitude that he meets, including those of his worldly enemies. His point of view, which I shall call "inclusiveness," thus seems near to a Christian one, for it counsels a tolerance that borders on Christian love. However, the hero does not love his neighbor for Jesus' sake but for the sake of filling his own consciousness with truth. Yet a kind of Christian humility is the end result of his attitude. Believing as he does that other people have an acquaintance with Life that is as valid as his own, and recognizing his relative unimportance in the great panorama that he sees, he is characterized above all by magnanimity. He believes in everything as a part of Life but in nothing as a final version of it.

In contrast, the Jamesian villain—I use the word only for want of a more accurate one—is "practical." Gilbert Osmond may be taken as a model of the type. He looks on society as a field of battle, and instead of seeking the truth he is concerned only to use his social weapons to best advantage. He may or may not have the intellectual and moral capacity for inclusiveness, but he finds it imprudent to train his sights beyond any immediate goal. His ends supposedly justify his means. On the level of the action his sin is an exploitation of the hero's inexperience and good faith. Metaphysically he is sinning against truth itself, for in effect he is attempting to deny the value of a disinterested zeal for knowledge. Inclusiveness and practicality are the opposite poles in a moral world whose supreme virtue is an open mind.

The Americans who appear in James's "international" novels have a more or less fixed set of possible roles in this contrast of values. The American is a visitor from a world of relative ingenuousness. His civilization is so young that it hasn't had time to develop social gestures that will represent its characteristic perceptions about reality. He is often inarticulate; he feels the tension created by his insufficient ability to express himself in terms that the European can understand. Christopher Newman in *The American* is the example most often cited, but any number of others could be mentioned. In Jamesian language they are "empty" of social refinements, while the European is full to overflowing with them. But human nature abhors a vacuum: the American often compensates for his spiritual loneliness with a "sacred rage," a reliance on moral righteousness instead of worldliness.

This righteousness can run in the broadest or narrowest channels. Christopher Newman is able to achieve a kind of magnanimity by virtue of his belief in his moral superiority to France, but Sarah Pocock in *The Ambassadors* uses the same conviction as a basis for the meanest sort of prejudice. In other characters—Madame de Mauves, for example—the American righteousness is treated with a deliberate moral ambivalence. Although we admire Madame de Mauves's firm integrity, we are left wondering at the end whether this very integrity may not be to blame for the unnecessary death of her husband. At any rate, there is an important similarity in the case of every American who has not renounced his nationality: he is incapable of living in an amoral, "realistic" manner. As Philip Rahv says, in a slightly different connection, "The principle of realism presupposes a thoroughly secularized relationship between the ego and experience."[5] Most Americans, even as ruthless businessmen, cannot be secular in this sense. They are always making moral estimates of their actions, always justifying or condemning themselves according to some unseen standard. At his best the American lives on principles; at his worst, on moralistic half-truths. He cannot cultivate emotions as a pastime, or relax in a bath of history and tradition. He is by definition intense.

In Europe the American is particularly reminded of his social homelessness. As a remedy he is inclined either to adopt a foreign pattern of social observances, as Gilbert Osmond does, or to intensify his moral strictness, as Waymarsh does in *The Ambassadors,* or to attempt a comprehensive grasp of everything he touches, by a special effort of his intellect or heart. In this third group are the truly inclusive heroes. If Europe offers the American a chance to renounce his country, it may also challenge him to fall back on the best qualities of his "empty" and hence uncorrupted American soul. It is revealing that while the morally purest characters in our three late novels are all Americans, in two cases the most unsavory characters are American as well. This whole situation will be seen to tie in with the philosophical problem raised by Madame Merle. The International Theme—naïve America versus sophisticated Europe—remains the context of James's drama, but the moral question becomes more complex as naïveté comes less and less to be regarded as a virtue in itself. Is purity of imagination compatible with the highest inclusive heroism? James raises this question with increasing stress in *The Ambassadors, The Wings of the Dove,* and *The*

5. Philip Rahv, *Image and Idea* (Norfolk, Conn., New Directions, 1949), p. 13.

Golden Bowl, and I feel that in each successive novel he moved closer to a full statement of his attitude.

2.

The plot of *The Ambassadors* centers about Chad Newsome, the rebellious heir to an unspecified industry in Woollett, Massachusetts, who has spurned his family and fortune and secluded himself in Paris, presumably in the clutches of an "evil woman." His widowed mother sends Lambert Strether, to whom she is informally engaged, to persuade Chad to accept his obligations. Instead of being reformed by Strether, an unexpectedly civilized Chad converts Strether to his own point of view. Strether himself falls in love, intellectually, with Chad's Madame de Vionnet, and for her sake actually prevents Chad from returning to Woollett with Mrs. Newsome's second platoon of ambassadors, the Pococks. Alienated from Mrs. Newsome and presented with the opportunity of marrying Maria Gostrey, an attractive woman who loves him, Strether nevertheless decides to return to America.

Lambert Strether is the hero of the book, and all the action is seen through his eyes. He is a widower of fifty-five who thinks that life has passed him by, as indeed it has, and when he gets to Europe he begins to understand what the trouble has been. Mrs. Newsome, the Woollett dowager who is paying for his trip, has very subtly dominated his mind with her own narrow outlook on life. Superficially she is all beneficence. By allowing him to edit a small review whose debts she pays, she provides him not only with a means of living but with a moderate portion of "fame" and "culture" as well. Furthermore, she intends to take the hero out of his financial misery for good, by marrying him. But once Strether has put some geographical and moral distance between himself and Mrs. Newsome he is able to see that her apparent generosity has had a restricting effect on his consciousness, and indeed that the whole society represented by Woollett, Massachusetts has restricted him. In Paris he is confronted with the image of a world which now seems at least as real as Woollett and a good deal more interesting; yet he has never had a chance to take it into account, for Woollett has had nothing to do with it. Strether, like Hyacinth, wants to know rather than to enjoy this new life—or more precisely, he wants to enjoy it only in order to know it. Paris becomes a symbol of everything he has felt lacking in himself, and he pursues the ideal of self-cultivation with religious fervor. It is too late to make his life over, but it is not too late to dedicate himself to an openness of spirit that he might have developed long ago, had he only suspected how large and various the world beyond Woollett actually was. James in his preface states the issue as it appears to Strether:

Would there yet perhaps be time for reparation?—reparation, that is, for the injury done his character; for the affront, he is quite ready to say, so stupidly put upon it and in which he has even himself had so clumsy a hand? The answer to which is that he now at all events *sees;* so that the business of .my tale and the march of my action, not to say the precious moral of everything, is just my demonstration of this process of vision.[6]

The result of the process of vision is inclusiveness.

Strether's career is morally parallel to Hyacinth's, and some idea of the degree of understatement in James's later method can be gained from the reflection that whereas Hyacinth pays for his vision with his life, Strether achieves exactly the same goal by merely deciding quietly not to accept the offer of a comfortable way of living. Although this is in some sense a neutralization of dramatic possibilities, it does bring the question of values into sharper focus than before. Strether's advanced age and his recurring awareness of it prevent us from confusing his moral growth with mere factionalism; he has nothing ultimately at stake but the expansion of his awareness of Life. In what James called the central passage in the book, as well as the inspiration for the whole, Strether makes a little speech about freedom which negates any hope of his own for a new start: "One's consciousness is poured—so that one 'takes' the form . . . and is more or less compactly held by it: one lives, in fine, as one can." (p. 150) Immediately afterward he exhorts the young American painter Bilham to cultivate the illusion of freedom, and later in the novel he thinks of Chad as free, but he can never forget for long that he himself is running out of time. In effect he defies his own deterministic philosophy by breaking out of his Woollett "mould," but his success is entirely on an intellectual, philosophical level.

6. *The Art of the Novel*, p. 308. In his prospectus of 1900 for *The Ambassadors*, James emphasized a more specific reason for Strether's seriousness. Many years previous to his "embassy" Strether had buried an adolescent son whom he had greatly misunderstood, through an unwillingness to make allowances for the boy's "strangeness." When the boy died Strether blamed his own narrow-mindedness for his son's unhappy life, and as a result he developed a compulsive desire to remind himself of his failure. "Deep and silent penance has he privately performed ever since." (*Notebooks*, p. 382) However, James does not stress this circumstance in the novel itself.

Strether meets the inevitable Jamesian confidante, Maria Gostrey, at the very outset upon his arrival in England, and the implicit contrast between Maria and Strether's companion from America, Waymarsh, immediately dramatizes the two extremes between which he will find himself for the rest of the novel. Waymarsh is a satiric figure throughout the book, but there are undertones of genuine respect in James's attitude toward him. He is a personification of New World austerity, simplicity, and discomfort. What Strether says of Woollett is also true of Waymarsh: he isn't sure he *ought* to enjoy things. In the eyes of Milrose, Connecticut, he leads a "full life," which is to say that he has narrowly escaped a nervous breakdown from overwork. His friends in Europe refer to him affectionately as "Sitting Bull," and his, specifically, is the sacred rage against the nice European distinctions which strike the democratic soul as invidious. All things foreign seem to him to be interconnected in a conspiracy against good will, as this reflection bears out: "The Catholic church, for Waymarsh—that was to say the enemy, the monster of bulging eyes and far-reaching, quivering, groping tentacles—was exactly society, exactly the multiplication of shibboleths, exactly the discrimination of types and tones, exactly the wicked old Rows of Chester, rank with feudalism; exactly, in short, Europe." (p. 29) He is as helpless and uneasy in Europe as a revival preacher in an art gallery. Everything should be either black or white; why all these intermediate shades?

Maria Gostrey represents an opposite attitude. She is an American who appears at first to have overcome every trait in the national character, through constant exposure to Europe. Yet her type is as genuine as Waymarsh's. James mentions in his notebook that "She is inordinately modern, the fruit of actual, international conditions, of the growing polyglot Babel."[7] She seems to be the perfectly adjusted expatriate, living for the cultivation of her tastes and the exercise of her sympathies. Her actual loneliness emerges only gradually, as we come to realize how dependent she is upon her role as Strether's guide. Strether recognizes at once the usefulness of her companionship, not merely as an aid in "seeing the sights," but in accustoming him to a European manner of thinking. In her presence he becomes more conscious than before of Waymarsh's shortcomings, and together they are amused—but also impressed—by his sacred rage. It would be stretching the point to say for Strether, as we could say for the influences

7. *Notebooks*, p. 378.

in Hyacinth's life, that he is composed of "Waymarsh-forces" and "Maria-forces." His two companions suggest, rather, his past and his future. Waymarsh's bluntness reminds him of the New England he is leaving behind, a New England he is increasingly tempted to regard in caricature. Maria's superior perceptiveness shows him the subtlety of the world he is about to enter. He is not really torn between Waymarsh and Maria; he gravitates instinctively to Maria.

This is an initial victory not directly for Europe but for the cause of self-cultivation. Strether has not yet realized that a commitment to the latter implies an acceptance of the former. His mental conflict at this early point is between Maria's worldliness and his sense of obligation to Mrs. Newsome. He too isn't sure he ought to enjoy things, and the fact that he is capable of being seduced by the Old World only sharpens his painful sense of duty. When he gets to Paris and begins to appreciate the attractiveness of the place, he alters his religious interpretation of his mission: "Was it at all possible, for instance, to like Paris enough without liking it too much? He luckily, however, hadn't promised Mrs. Newsome not to like it at all. He was ready to recognize at this stage that such an engagement *would* have tied his hands. . . . The only engagement he had taken, when he looked the thing in the face, was to do what he reasonably could." (p. 62) Shortly afterward he has gone much further: "He wasn't there to dip, to consume—he was there to reconstruct. He wasn't there for his own profit—not, that is, the direct; he was there on some chance of feeling the brush of the wing of the stray spirit of youth." (p. 65) This process of compromise and revision is going on, largely between the lines, from the first day of Strether's acquaintance with Maria. He finds himself ashamed to tell her that he is from no more outstanding a home than Woollett, Massachusetts. (p. 11) When she asks if Mrs. Newsome is in Europe, he expresses relief that she is safely isolated at home. And when he dines with Maria he is given over to "uncontrolled perceptions" (p. 36), which add up to the conclusion that Maria's company is strikingly different from, and more exciting than, that of Mrs. Newsome. From the point of view of sensuous appeal, Maria and Europe seem to be winning the battle hands down.

But Strether is not so easily wooed. Before he has met Chad he remains convinced that however provincial Mrs. Newsome may appear, her moral ideas and purpose are completely sound. To think that Strether's eye immediately dictates to his heart is to forget the basic

Puritan distrust of the flesh; for Strether is, in spite of himself, a descendant of the Puritans. This is brought out only in suggestion, but the suggestions are deliberate and important. Strether's sense of sin is out of all proportion to his sins. Like Mrs. Newsome ("to lie was beyond her art"; p. 66) he looks upon his vows as sacred obligations. Witness, for example, his need to rationalize his enjoyment of Europe, even on the most innocent level. He has, as he later accuses himself, an "odious ascetic suspicion of any form of beauty." (p. 133) Even his vocabulary shows traces of Calvinism. For example, Chad appeals to him as a "pagan," though a pagan whom Woollett would do well to tolerate. Waymarsh, the personified survival of New England's fiercest asceticism, is called a "Hebrew prophet" (p. 79) by his English benefactress, Miss Barrace. Strether's apparent shift of allegiance can be viewed in part as a movement from a Calvinistic to a more secular view of human pleasures.

Strether's perceptions are no less restricted by his background than Hyacinth's were. At first, to Maria Gostrey's considerable amusement, all things European strike him as elegant and grand. And he begins with none of Maria's talent for the crucial business of guessing what the other characters are thinking. But with Maria's help he gradually learns to make the proper distinctions, and by the middle of the book his judgment has been so improved that he can find his way through the maze of true and false hints with no aid at all. However, it is significant that his moral background, in fixing his interpretation of the word "virtue," prevents him from grasping the most important—and to Maria's mind the most obvious—fact about Madame de Vionnet's attachment to Chad. Strether is constantly forced to temper the extremity of his values, for Paris is a place where "what seemed all surface one moment seemed all depth the next." (p. 62) It defies the compartmentalizing mind. Before the city is through with Strether he will have admitted by implication that all his previous beliefs were mere prejudices, and the fact that he does so with an acquiescence approaching zeal proves not only that he is covetous of the truth, but also that as an American he is thoroughly aware of his emptiness. Once he has been emancipated from a few superstitions there is nothing left to sustain him in the comfortable belief that his ideas at any given point correspond to realities. The very earnestness with which he denounces Woollett can be traced to an insufficiency that Woollett instilled in him. His inadequacies spur him on to deeper penetrations, just as, in a lesser sense, Waymarsh's inadequacies lead to grander gestures of defiance. There is something distinctly noble in such reactions. It is what Maria means when she says, "We're abysmal—but may we never fill up!" (p. 295)

The pervasive *motif* of youth versus age, of hovering opportunity and lost opportunity, crystallizes in Strether's acquaintance with "Little Bilham," Chad's companion. While Chad is conveniently absent from Paris, Maria's task of "softening up" the ambassador is transferred to Bilham. James suggests this schematic arrangement in the last paragraph of Part II, before Strether has so much as spoken to Bilham. Maria is still in England, so that ". . . Waymarsh . . . struck him as the present alternative to the young man [Bilham] in the balcony. When he did move it was fairly to escape that alternative. Taking his way over the streets at last and passing through the *porte-cochère* of the house was like consciously leaving Waymarsh out." (p. 68) In other words, Strether symbolically rejects Waymarsh's manner of life in preference to an ideal first embodied in Maria and now to be represented by Bilham.

His attitude toward Bilham is friendly but equivocal. Bilham reminds him of his own youth, and Bilham's case history contains an interesting parallel to his own. They are both artists in temperament, but both have despaired of producing works of art. Strether has always lamented his failure, but Bilham is distinctly different. He is both "intense" and "serene" in Strether's eyes.

It was by little Bilham's amazing serenity that he had been at first affected, but he had inevitably, in his circumspection, felt it as the trail of the serpent, the corruption, as he might conveniently have said, of Europe; whereas the promptness with which it came up for Miss Gostrey as but a special little form of the oldest thing they knew justified it, to his own vision as well, on the spot. He wanted to be able to like his specimen with a clear good conscience, and this fully permitted it. What had muddled him was precisely the small artist-man's way—it was so complete—of being more American than anybody. [pp. 86f.]

If Bilham is an "abysmal" American, he no longer shows it. His is an unusual case, and one whose characteristically American quality James does not bother to explain. He is serene, paradoxically, by virtue of his emptiness. "The amiable youth, then, looked out, as it had first struck Strether, at a world in respect to which he hadn't a prejudice. The one our friend most instantly missed was the usual one in favor of an occupation accepted. Little Bilham had an occupation, but it was only an occupation declined; and it was by his general exemption from alarm, anxiety, or remorse on this score that the impression of his serenity was made." (p. 87) Bilham had come to Paris in the first place to learn how to paint, but like many another prospective artist he found that his high standards of taste prevented him from taking his own work seriously: "his productive power faltered in proportion as his knowledge grew." (p. 87) Thus his unwillingness to paint suggests something more than a personal inadequacy; it is a form of tribute to the Old Masters. Although "he had not saved from his shipwreck a scrap of anything but his beautiful intelligence and his confirmed habit of Paris" (p. 87), these things suffice. He is content to exchange most of the ordinary comforts of life for the privilege of collecting knowledge passively, of seeing Life as a disinterested spectator. His implicit philosophy is that to *live* one's vision of Life, in the strictest sense and concerning the broadest vision, involves abstaining from *doing* things at all.

This thrusts us into an area where James is not generally considered to be on firm ground. Few critics are willing to see any sort of idleness as a virtue. Bilham's case is only one of three in *The Ambassadors*, the other "idlers" being Chad and eventually Strether himself. We cannot attempt to justify or condemn James's position—if indeed it is his position—until all the evidence has been taken into account. But it should be apparent already that James is not dealing with industry versus laziness, but with ways of seeing. Bilham, like Hyacinth, is mentally active by virtue of being uncommitted to a narrowing form of life. His "activity" is the exercise of his expansive imagination, which he refuses to compromise. The intensity which I have called a necessary term in the definition of an American operates here in a new way: it reinforces an essentially European manner of living.

However, there is nothing truly European about Bilham. By virtue of his intensity he is "one of us," as Maria announces. This is why Strether is interested in seeing him make the most of his life. Strether understands the national want of fulfillment, and he knows from his own example that the way to profit from Life is not to watch it drifting away from you. He passionately exhorts Bilham not to "miss things," and later on he urges him to get married, first to Jeanne de Vionnet and then, when that appears unlikely, to Mamie Pocock. He wants Bilham to participate in, not merely observe, the great panorama, for participation is the richest means of seeing. The heart as well as the mind must be involved. No one is able to capture Life in its totality, in Strether's view, but everyone is entitled to try, and the only way to succeed moderately is to make a full-scale effort. The central passage of the book, already quoted in part, makes Strether's position clear:

"The affair—I mean the affair of life—couldn't . . . have been different for me; for it's, at the best, a tin mould, either fluted and embossed, with ornamental excrescences, or else smooth and dreadfully plain, into which, a helpless jelly, one's consciousness is poured—so that one 'takes' the form . . . and is more or less compactly held by it . . . Still, one has the illusion of freedom; therefore don't be, like me, without the memory of that illusion. I was either, at the right time, too stupid or too intelligent to have it; I don't quite know which." [p. 150]

Although at any given point one is no better than his past circumstances have made him, he nevertheless has had a measure of influence over those circumstances. If one admits at the start that he has no hope of escaping the bounds of his education, he will be likely to despair of making that education as complete as it might be. "The illusion of freedom" can carry one along to something very close to actual freedom—an exposure to circumstances so various that any single mould will no longer determine one's sense of truth. The "fluted and embossed" mould can be construed as the refined, Parisian way of life, and the "smooth and dreadfully plain" one as Woollett's. Neither is substantially larger than the other. Paris, indeed, provides an incentive for making fine distinctions, but it also provides a kind of ready-made smugness, an attitude of moral neutrality speciously derived from "experience." The beauty of the American's life in Europe is that he can, if he so chooses, gather knowledge of a more complicated world than his own without abandoning his basic sense of values. Unlike the American in America he is encouraged to exercise his taste, and unlike the native European he can be directed in his self-cultivation by a clear awareness of his needs. But as Strether insists, he must aspire not merely to understand but to become a part of the Life he sees.

Although Bilham is perceptibly influenced by Strether and is anxious to take his advice, it is the younger man who seems to do most of the influencing. This relationship is curious. The fact that Bilham reminds Strether of his own younger days not only provokes Strether to forewarn him, it turns Strether himself toward Bilham's present way of thinking. He has found his "chance of feeling the brush of the wing of the stray spirit of youth." By the moment of Chad's appearance on the scene Strether has realized that his association with Maria, with Europe, with Bilham, and even, by contrast, with Waymarsh, has left him "quite, already, in Chad's hands." (p. 92) Bilham's presence has been the decisive influence, and Strether's knowledge that this was premeditated by Chad only makes Chad himself seem all the more remarkable. Bilham has graciously introduced Strether to Chad's unexpectedly well-mannered and agreeable form of life, and by means of his extreme tact he has discouraged all embarrassing questions about Chad's private affairs. As Strether tries to explain to Waymarsh—and this is evidence of Europe's superiority in conversational battle—"You can't make out over here what people do know." (p. 75) This inspires a classic outburst of Waymarsh's, ending in the precept, "People don't take a fine-tooth comb to groom a horse." (p. 75) Waymarsh sees a simple case of adultery as the essence of the matter, and doesn't consider it worth the soiling of honest hands to intervene. But Strether's thinking has been diverted from such lines. When Chad arrives, sophisticated and genial, the ambassador is already somewhat ashamed of his mission.

Chad's character is left ambiguous until the story is almost over. What we see is his high European polish, his ability to control any situation with good-natured delicacy. He was, we are told, a "brute," a "monster" of willfulness before he went abroad. The unspoken question in Strether's mind, when he sees him so altered in manner, is whether he has really changed inwardly. By degrees Chad convinces him that he has. This is easy for Chad in the same way that it was easy for Osmond to impress Isabel and for the Princess to impress Hyacinth: being unfamiliar with Chad's continental manners, Strether has no way of telling true nobility from false. He has been prepared to argue with Chad on frank American terms, but he finds to his dismay that Chad has adopted a different set of rules—rules of good manners which Strether can only admire and fall victim to. "You could deal with a man as himself—you couldn't deal with him as somebody else." (p. 94)

Favorably inclined as he has now become to a world where surfaces and depths seem interchangeable, Strether is greatly impressed by Chad's social developments. Even on the level of simple physical appearance the changes seem uniformly to be for the better:

Chad was brown and thick and strong, and, of old, Chad had been rough. Was all the difference therefore that he was actually smooth? Possibly; for that he *was* smooth was as marked as in the taste of a sauce or in the rub of a hand. The effect of it was general—it had retouched his features, drawn them with a cleaner line. It had cleared his eyes and settled his color and polished his fine square teeth—the main ornament of his face; and at the same time that it had given him a form and a surface, almost a design, it had toned his voice, established his accent, encouraged his smile to more play and his other motions to less. He had formerly, with a great deal of action, expressed very little; and he now expressed whatever was necessary with almost none at all. It was as if, in short, he had really, copious perhaps, but shapeless, been put into a firm mould and turned successfully out. [p. 104]

This last sentence should come to the reader's mind when he meets Strether's slightly later sermon on moulds, fluted and plain. The implicit question is this: does Strether's identical image for describing Chad and describing the limitations of human consciousness mean that he is aware of the restrictions of Chad's new "form"? The answer is perhaps both yes and no. In his clearest moments Strether knows that Chad is no freer in the strictly metaphysical sense of the word. His new manner is the stamp of a mould like any other. Still, Strether has been carefully brought around to a feeling that Chad's new form is far superior to his old one—or rather, to his previous lack of one. Chad is perfectly adapted to his environment, and the environment in question appears to Strether, at his present stage of awareness, as a whole universe of wonders. He believes in Chad's metamorphosis so thoroughly that at times he thinks of him specifically as "free": "His changed state, his lovely home, his beautiful things, his easy talk . . . what were such marked matters all but the notes of his freedom?" (p. 114) It would be unfair to say that Strether means exactly "free will" here. Compared to his old self Chad *is* free—he is free *from* his old self—and it is this comparison that seems uppermost in Strether's mind.

From this point onward the novel becomes an elaborate guessing game, a detective story whose mysteries are expressed in, and approached by means of, the slightest outward hints. Strether perceives that Chad is "a man marked out by women," and the chief mystery thus becomes "what woman or women?" The field is soon narrowed to two, Madame de Vionnet and her daughter Jeanne. Strether first suspects Jeanne of being Chad's beloved, but this error, fostered by Chad and Madame de Vionnet, is quickly rejected. It is Madame de

Vionnet herself, a middle-aged woman with no immediate air of distinction, who has "formed" Chad. She appears to be genuinely in love with him, and the reader assumes that her affection is returned. When this much has been established in Strether's mind, Chad has only to convince him of Madame de Vionnet's worthiness in order to convert him utterly to his own point of view.

This is accomplished by Madame de Vionnet herself, and with the greatest of ease. Strether's gradual progression from a Puritan to an Epicurean frame of mind has weakened him for the final assault. Madame de Vionnet, as he discovers when his first impression of her has faded, is the epitome of civilized Gallic taste. Her taste is so sure that she rarely feels obliged to display it in public. As James remarks in his prospectus for the novel, the cleverest thing about her is that she does not seem "dazzlingly clever."[8] Her art lies in masking things so casually, with such an appearance of consistent frankness, that few or no traces of the hidden facts can be found; or, when forced into a corner, she can admit the bald and unpleasant truth with such delicacy that her inquisitor can be charmed out of his anger. "As she presented things the ugliness—goodness knew why—went out of them; none the less too that she could present them, with an art of her own, by not so much as touching them." (p. 398) She is a master at conversational politics, not merely in her easy duplicity but also in her manner of gently forcing people to pledge their allegiance to her. Strether in particular finds himself unable to resist her pleas for help. Such promises cost Madame de Vionnet a secret or two, but nothing that would seriously compromise her. She so impresses Strether with the difficulty of her own plight—caught as she is between Mrs. Newsome's pressure on Chad and, as we come to suspect, Chad's own business ambitions— that Strether ignores his own equally urgent predicament. He too is trapped; his indebtedness to Mrs. Newsome cannot be reconciled with his growing sympathy with the Frenchwoman. Strether, who has learned some duplicity himself, originally has no intention of keeping his promise to "save" Madame de Vionnet, as close attention to the motivation of his vow will bear out: "So it was that the way to meet her—and the way, as well, in a manner, to get off—came over him. He heard himself use the exorbitant word, the very sound of which helped to determine his flight. 'I'll save you if I can.' " (p. 177) He is convinced at this point that he *cannot* save her. But Madame de Vionnet,

8. *Notebooks*, p. 392.

in James's image, drives the golden nail in a little farther at each opportunity, until Strether finds himself securely fastened and no longer minding it.

The thing especially to note in their relationship is that Strether is fully conscious of being "used" by his adversary. It is just her masterful way of ensnaring him that he admires. His reaction to her is aesthetic rather than moral, but his new dedication to "taste" is applied with a kind of moral earnestness. He fills up his social vacuum by placing good manners above everything else, including his self-interest—something that few Europeans, however cultured, would think of doing. Strether knows well enough that manners can be used for selfish ends. He simply doesn't care, as Waymarsh does, to conclude that all manners are base or noble according only to the ends in mind. The end in this case, the continuation of a love affair of dubious propriety, interests Strether far less than the tactics that Chad and Madame de Vionnet are employing with him. But if one decided that means justify ends for Strether, he would be thinking more schematically than Strether himself does. At this stage he is not entirely aware of the moral issue: he lets his "taste" blind him to it. This is a fault, no doubt, but it is not the same as saying that he is frankly condoning adultery.

It is tempting to regard this phase of Strether's development, in which he has become even more Gallic than Chad in moral outlook, as an ethical nadir. Certainly he has suffered from having abandoned one moral system without fully understanding its substitute. But some critics have gone further and said that this mistake is a sign of insufficiency in *The Ambassadors* as a whole. Yvor Winters, for example, inveighs against James for bothering with the idle, worthless existence of Chad in Paris, and is especially disappointed with Strether for being so impressed by him. Chad, Winters says, is not worth "the expenditure of quite so much moral heroism as Strether expends upon him." "The central issue," he concludes, "does not quite support the dramatics."[9] This statement is based on the mistaken assumption that nothing more is at stake than the future career of Chad Newsome. The issue is ethical, and of the highest order: it is the relationship of principle to taste. Winters would probably say, with Waymarsh, that principle transcends taste, and that it is immoral to think otherwise. Madame de Vionnet might be said to exemplify the possibility that taste may replace principle. But where does Strether stand? This, I submit, is the most difficult

9. Yvor Winters, *Maule's Curse* (Norfolk, Conn., New Directions, 1938), p. 206.

and crucial problem in the book. Although Strether's values at this point are still imperfectly formed, we can get some idea of his position by reviewing his opinion of the three characters who are contending for his approval.

Very little can be said in behalf of Mrs. Newsome. The fact that she never appears in person and yet is ever present in the minds of the New England characters makes us feel her almost as an abstract force, a principle of repression. Her correspondence with Strether, which seems so friendly and patient at first, begins to take on sinister overtones when we realize that he is being subtly compelled to justify all of his actions, and indeed his thoughts, according to her particular standards. She is the mythical figure we have come to recognize as "Mom"—"a *moral swell*" (p. 47), as Maria calls her. She "doesn't admit surprises." (p. 358) In contrast to her intensely abysmal countrymen she is "filled as full, packed as tight, as she'll hold." (p. 358) Strether eventually decides that there is but one way to deal successfully with her: "You've got morally and intellectually to get rid of her." (p. 358) And with her goes Woollett, Massachusetts, and its habit of narrow moralizing.

Chad and Madame de Vionnet are not so easily judged. One thing is certain: Chad has derived great benefit from her love. Although Yvor Winters suggests that she has corrupted Chad's values,[10] quite the opposite is true, as everyone in the novel except Sarah Pocock is perfectly able to recognize. Chad has been transformed from a nasty young adventurer into a gentleman. Whatever sense of obligation he has acquired, whatever tact and decency and tolerance are due to Madame de Vionnet's deliberate influence. Furthermore, these developments are not accompanied by any of the overtones James is so adept at suggesting in a relationship where one party is guilty of tyrannizing another's mind. Madame de Vionnet has "freed" Chad, and even though she wants his presence desperately, she will give him up rather than use his real indebtedness to her as a means of keeping him. When Strether learns that Chad is ready to desert her and return to Woollett, the case for America's symbolic value looks extremely poor. As Elizabeth Stevenson puts it—although perhaps too neatly— "In this novel the young American is the cruel exploiter, and the older, experienced European woman is the gentle victim."[11]

By the time the Pococks, Mrs. Newsome's second-string ambassa-

10. *Ibid.*, p. 184.
11. Elizabeth Stevenson, *The Crooked Corridor* (New York, Macmillan, 1949), p. 60.

dors, have descended upon Paris, Strether has his conclusions about the above relationships well in mind. He feels that Chad owes everything to Madame de Vionnet, and that neither he nor Chad owes anything to Mrs. Newsome. He expects that the arrival of Sarah and Jim Pocock, Chad's sister and brother-in-law, and Mamie Pocock, Jim's sister and Chad's prospective wife, will bring only confusion and ill feeling. America's symbolic fortunes may be said to take an upward turn when Strether meets the Pococks and finds them not so fierce after all. Furthermore, he is immediately reminded of Mrs. Newsome's special forgotten charm, which these envoys seem somehow able to project:

> The woman at home, the woman to whom he was attached, was before him just long enough to give him again the measure of the wretchedness, in fact really of the shame, of their having to recognize the formation, between them, of a "split." He had taken this measure in solitude and meditation; but the catastrophe, as Sarah steamed up, looked, for its few seconds, unprecedentedly dreadful—or proved, more exactly, absolutely unthinkable; so that his finding something free and familiar to respond to brought with it an instant renewal of his loyalty. He had suddenly sounded the whole depth, had gasped at what he might have lost. [pp. 252f.]

This reversal is only temporary, however. Its real function is to remind Strether and ourselves of how much is at stake in his decision to defend Madame de Vionnet. Sarah Pocock, who is less sophisticated than her mother but is essentially a faithful embodiment of her mother's attitudes, quickly loses Strether's sympathy by refusing to see that Chad's new virtues are due to Madame de Vionnet's care. She looks upon that lady as a kind of sorceress, and upon Strether as a bewitched apprentice. When Sarah blithely insists that she "knows" Paris, as if the city were only an assortment of tourist attractions, Strether's revulsion becomes complete. America as represented by Sarah soon falls back into disrepute.

Mamie's effect is more impressive. She too evokes old and pleasant sentiments. "There were positively five minutes in which the last word seemed of necessity to abide with a Woollett represented by a Mamie." (p. 253) But Mamie, unlike Sarah, stands for something to which Strether is permanently rather than occasionally dedicated. This is our friend, the abysmal American soul: "he felt satisfied that her consciousness was, after all, empty for its size, rather too simple than too mixed, and that the kind way with her would be not to take many things out of it, but to put as many as possible in." (p. 254) Strether finds Mamie quite able to stand a comparison with her French contemporary, Jeanne de Vionnet. Jeanne is perfectly bred and charmingly innocent, in the sincerely lifeless way that only convent-educated girls can be innocent. Mamie's innocence is of a richer and fuller sort. She faces every situation honestly and realistically, regardless of its hazards. Jeanne, by contrast, is all fragility and discretion. The difference is something like that between a sunflower and a lily; if not the lovelier of the two, Mamie is unquestionably the taller and sturdier. But she finds herself rendered no less helpless by Chad's new manners than Strether was. She is able to perceive at a glance that Chad has altered for the better, and she lets the implications of this fact influence her so deeply that she relinquishes her claim to him. She sees that Madame de Vionnet has already accomplished her project of "reforming" Chad, and that he is no longer in need of her maternal patience. Mamie's saving grace, in Strether's eyes, is that her sense of justice is stronger than her Woollett prudishness. Evil or not, Madame de Vionnet has done wonders for Chad, and once Mamie has seen him she never for a moment entertains the evangelical notion of converting him back to "Americanism."

This is a blow to Strether, who has never before realized the degree of incompatibility between Chad's world and Mamie's. Believing as he still does in the "virtuous attachment," he has hoped that a match between Chad and Mamie would reconcile the opposing parties. Indeed, he sees it as his own last opportunity for a reconciliation. But there is no more chance of converting Mamie to Chad's ways than there appears to be of converting Chad back to Mamie's. The ocean flows between them. Admiring Mamie in spite of his general sympathy with the French attitude, Strether hesitates at moments between the two. His association with Jim Pocock at this point reinforces his attachment to Woollett in a unique way. Jim, to be sure, is easygoing and empty headed, and his immediate approval of Chad's cause provides little more than comic relief. He has no influence with his moralistic wife, and no conception of the values at stake. But he sees the affair on a marvelously simple level that Strether concedes to be at least partly justified by the facts. As Strether explains, "He understands . . . that Chad and I have above all wanted to have a good time, and his view is simple and sharp. Nothing will persuade him—in the light, that is, of my behavior—that I really didn't, quite as much as Chad, come over to have one before it was too late. He wouldn't have expected it of me; but men of my age, at Woollett—and especially the least likely ones— have been noted as liable to strange outbreaks, belated, uncanny clutches at the unusual, the ideal." (p. 284) Jim is himself a caricatured example of the type, and insofar as Strether is forced to agree that Jim's escape is similar to his own, he must disbelieve in the absolute, almost occult significance of Paris. When he begins to think of his whole adventure as an outlet for grievances, a binge, the desire is reborn in him to get back to simple American realities. His hope of matching Bilham and Mamie is offered as a kind of expiation, a reaffirming of Woollett's moral power: "I've been sacrificing so to strange gods that I feel I want to put on record, somehow, my fidelity—fundamentally unchanged, after all—to our own." (p. 319)

This "return to religion" is also inspired in part by his disgust at the news of Jeanne de Vionnet's impending marriage to a French nobleman whom he has never met, and whom Jeanne knows scarcely better. He learns that Chad has been instrumental in arranging the match, a marriage of pure convenience on Madame de Vionnet's side in more respects than one. Strether's reaction is twofold. In the first place, the impersonal handling of the affair gives him an immediate sense of the potential cruelty of custom. The question of whether Jeanne loves her fiancé is, despite Madame de Vionnet's assurances, left open, and we never know for certain that she hasn't loved Chad all along. Strether is burdened with the sense that this fine, delicate creature is being sold for the sake of a title. Nothing could be more appalling to the romantic American soul. Strether feels for the first time that he has probed through the veil of manners and reached their ugly significance: "He had allowed for depths, but these were greater: and it was as if, oppressively—indeed absurdly—he was responsible for what they had now thrown up to the surface. It was—through something ancient and cold in it—what he would have called the real thing." (p. 291) Strether is now jolted from his faith in the interchangeability of surfaces and depths. He has finally allowed his idea of evil to settle upon the French as well as the American way of doing things.

The other result of the news is similar. Strether is suddenly aware that Chad and Madame de Vionnet are unscrupulous in the exercise of their social powers. It is convenient for them to have Jeanne safely married, especially if, as is quite possible, she really is in love with

Chad.[12] Looking backward, we can see that they have "used" her all along, first as a decoy to confuse Strether, and then as an example of French purity to impress (unsuccessfully) Sarah Pocock. This is all fair and normal in Madame de Vionnet's moral world, as Strether reluctantly observes. But he has not expected to find that Chad, the American, is not only an accomplice to the cynical marriage but actually its most diligent promoter. At this point Chad begins to take on some of the sinister hues of Gilbert Osmond.

Madame de Vionnet attempts to justify the matter to Strether by hinting that Jeanne is, after all, better off reasonably married than she would have been as a spinster pining away for Chad. Strether himself should supposedly approve of the match, for it ought to allay his fears that Jeanne is being undeservedly left out of things. But this line of heartless rationalization does not produce the desired effect. When Madame de Vionnet intimates that the marriage was arranged partly in order to please Strether himself, he is more enlightened and disturbed than ever. "Thus she could talk to him of what, of her innermost life— for that was what it came to—he must 'accept'; thus she could extraordinarily speak as if, in such an affair, his being satisfied had an importance. It was all a wonder, and it made the whole case larger." (p. 292) At the end of this conversation Strether is at least persuaded that everyone's convenience has been considered; but until this time he hadn't suspected that everyone's convenience *should* be considered in the marriage of one's daughter. The scene ends on a note of high tension. Madame de Vionnet has realized that Strether has been temporarily, perhaps permanently disillusioned with her methods, and Strether in his turn is on the brink of condoning or condemning Chad.

With one major exception, the stage has now been set for the climactic scene. The exception is Sarah Pocock's blunt ultimatum to Strether. With what would appear to be subtle wisdom Chad has placed the question of his staying or leaving entirely in Strether's hands. James suggests in his prospectus that this is simply the result of having worked Strether over to Chad's side, but in the novel itself a quite different motive is ascribed. Chad is weary of carrying the burden of

12. It is conceivable that Jeanne, loving Chad but taking in the extremity of her mother's predicament, willingly sacrifices herself by professing enthusiasm for her marriage to another man. But James never suggests it, and I am not sure that Jeanne possesses such strength of will. In any case her unblinking obedience to *maman* produces the desired results.

choice. He has already made up his mind that he wants to return to
Woollett and go into business; ironically enough, it has been his contact with Strether that has turned his thoughts homeward, but Strether's
admiration for Madame de Vionnet that has kept him in France.
Morally Chad is obligated both to Madame de Vionnet and to his
mother, but much more strongly and immediately to the former.
Strether can not only save him from returning if he wants to stay, he can
"force" him to return, thus saving him the embarrassment of breaking
openly with Madame de Vionnet on his own initiative. Chad is really
hoping that Strether will decree his return. He puts his fate in Strether's
hands not simply because he wants to leave—for he must surely be
aware that Strether wants him to stay—but because his own hands are
tied. Strether is his only hope of success. When Strether is, as a consequence, faced with a direct assault from Sarah, her outburst against his
hesitation imprints on his mind an indelible image of the crudity of
spirit that she and Mrs. Newsome represent. In short, he has been disillusioned with Woollett once and for all.

The discovery that Chad really wants to go home is another important step in Strether's disappointment with him, and yet it helps
Strether to judge him realistically. In his opinion anyone who cannot
see the full importance of Madame de Vionnet's gift is sadly deficient
in imagination. He has placed Mrs. Newsome and Sarah on this list,
and now he finds that he must include Chad himself. But this does
serve to clear Chad of the suspicion of evil intentions. He is devoid of
a moral imagination of either good or evil. Chad has a natural assertive-
ness and charm which, tempered by his new command of manners,
serve his interests as it were automatically, without his ever deliberately
planning to hurt others. He more or less inadvertently inspires good
faith. Maria sums it up: "There's nothing so magnificent—for making
others feel you—as to have no imagination." (p. 359) In the symbolic
battle between Paris and Woollett this is a further gain for Paris, for
Strether now feels that no one is doing justice to Madame de Vionnet,
including Chad. Then again, he is reminded by Chad's blindness that
Madame de Vionnet's achievement has not been so complete as he once
thought. The issue has reached a stalemate, and Strether, exhausted
with fixing his ideals first on one party and then another, takes a train
into the country for a day's rest.

Here, in one of James's truly great scenes, Strether finds Chad and
Madame de Vionnet together under circumstances which imply their

physical intimacy discreetly but irrefutably. Strether has been made increasingly aware of the true state of affairs, but this comes as a tremendous shock. "He recognized at last that he had really been trying, all along, to suppose nothing. Verily, verily, his labor had been lost. He found himself supposing everything." (p. 389) What this self-deception had signified was an effort to reconcile Woollett and Paris by means of the "virtuous attachment" theory; if Madame de Vionnet were truly disinterested, she could deserve the approval of Strether's chaste New England moral sense. Madame de Vionnet is not at all disinterested, and Strether realizes with a jolt that the fact of adultery has in itself no moral connotations for her. France must be deemed amoral even in the most liberal American perspective. The question hence becomes: is Strether going to condone Madame de Vionnet's amorality because she is French, and in deference to her civilizing influence, or is he going to condemn her flatly as a sinner?

While Strether is still in a condition of spiritual numbness from his discovery, he finds himself an actor in a delicate social comedy, the author and heroine of which is Madame de Vionnet. Instead of recognizing the obvious fact that she and Chad have been "found out," she plays her part to the hilt, pretending that she and her "good friend" have merely been passing a harmless afternoon in the country, not a whole weekend. Unfortunately, some of the essential props are absent, and all three actors are aware that the presentation is unconvincing. Still, by maintaining her pretense Madame de Vionnet gains a kind of triumph over the laws of evidence and logic. Looking back on it, Strether sees that her performance has been heroic rather than cowardly, and in a sense, in spite of everything, disinterested. She has preserved the decorum of the situation out of an innate respect for decorum itself: "He perceived soon enough at least that, however reasonable she might be, she was not vulgarly confused, and it herewith pressed upon him that their eminent 'lie,' Chad's and hers, was simply . . . such an inevitable tribute to good taste as he couldn't have wished them not to render. . . . once more and yet once more, he could trust her. That is he could trust her to make deception right." (p. 398)

This is Madame de Vionnet's saving grace, and it is not so immoral as it may sound. Strether now has it clearly in mind that the essential human relationships are not much different in Paris than in Woollett. The real difference is that whereas Woollett has refused to admit their existence, Paris has learned how to clothe them acceptably and live with

them. Strether's sympathy leans toward Madame de Vionnet in spite
of all he has learned. This sympathy is firmly and finally sanctioned
when Madame de Vionnet confesses to him, in her wonderfully circum-
spect way, how thoroughly she loves Chad, and reluctantly begs him
not to take Chad away. She realizes that such a decision will alienate
Strether from his old world, and she shows a genuine sense of guilt
at her persistence: "What I hate is myself—when I think that one has
to take so much, to be happy, out of the lives of others, and that one
isn't happy even then. . . . The wretched self is always there, always
making one somehow a fresh anxiety. What it comes to is that it's
not, that it's never, a happiness, any happiness at all, to *take*. The only
safe thing is to give." (pp. 401f.) This defines the real poignancy of her
situation. She is and has always been sensitive to her impositions on
Strether and to the fact that she has been keeping Chad in Paris against
his will. In fact, she seems to grasp these things more surely than the
benefits which atone for them. Her dilemma is that she can see the un-
reasonableness of her demands and yet simultaneously feel driven by
her love for Chad to persist in them. She has watched her sense of
ethics fall victim to her passion, and she suffers for it. When Strether
shows his awareness that her equilibrium hangs by the slender thread
of Chad's not deserting her, she breaks into tears, "giving up all
attempt at a manner." (p. 403) This is the final proof of her humanity.
Her love, "mature, abysmal,[13] pitiful" (p. 404), when considered with
the hopelessness of her future and her consciousness of having enlightened Strether too much for his own good, transforms her into a
pathetic figure: "he could see her there as vulgarly troubled . . . as a
maidservant crying for her young man. The only thing was that she
judged herself as the maidservant wouldn't; the weakness of which
wisdom too, the dishonor of which judgment, seemed but to sink her
lower." (p. 404) Her tears not only betray her despair, they remove
Strether's last trace of belief that surfaces and depths can really be in-
terchanged. Paris, the town of surfaces only, is now as far from being

13. The key word "abysmal" here suggests to me that Madame de Vionnet is in some
sense "American" in spirit. Her strong love for Chad provides her with an intensity
which, while it can hardly be classified as a sacred rage, nevertheless deprives her of the
common European confusion of manners and morals. She, no less than Waymarsh and
much more than Strether, is able to recognize that means do not really justify ends. The
fact that her means are graceful does not convince her that they atone in any way for
her less praiseworthy ends. Of all the characters in the book she is the most dispassionately
severe in judging herself.

an image of reality as Woollett is. Strether has been left high and dry, a man without a home.

This is not to say that he rates Paris and Woollett equally as places in which to live. Paris in this respect is still a fairyland, and Woollett more than ever a penal colony. Furthermore, it is fair to say that the French heroine has attracted more of his admiration—his love, in fact —than any American character has. This is not the point at all. What really matters is that Strether, like Hyacinth, has found that neither of his potential homes is large enough to accommodate his sense of reality. That sense has been nursed by Paris and stunted by Woollett, and in this respect the book is "anti-American." Also, his previous belief that the "real" people, in contrast to merely "well-mannered" people, are all Americans has crumbled in his discovery of Madame de Vionnet's sensitive conscience and Chad's lack of it. But the central judgment of the novel is that both systems are inadequate. Neither Woollett's abstemious Puritanism nor Paris' amoral secularism can account for the sense of Life that Strether has achieved through the expansion of his social and moral awareness.

Strether ends his adventure in controversial fashion. Maria Gostrey has hinted that she would accept a proposal of marriage from him. Nothing seems to stand in the way of Strether's proposing, least of all his natural inclination, yet he announces instead that he will return to America, for the peculiar reason that he feels he shouldn't "get anything" out of his embassy. Some critics look upon this as simple ingratitude. Winters, whose desire to expose the guilty obliges him to read James on the lowest level, calls Strether's return a "sacrifice of morality to appearances," "so that he may not seem in Woollett to have got anything for himself from a situation in which he will seem to his friends in Woollett to have betrayed his trust."[14] Calmer observers (F. O. Matthiessen, for example) suspect that Strether here betrays an instinctive resurgence of Puritan sentiment in reaction to Europe's corruption. But the most reliable authority on the subject, to my mind, is James himself in his prospectus:

He *can't* accept or assent. He won't. He doesn't. It's too late. It mightn't have been, sooner—but it is, yes, distinctly, now. He has come so far through his total little experience that he has come out on the other side—on the other side, even, of a union with Miss Gostrey. He must go back as he came—or rather,

14. *Maule's Curse,* p. 207.

really, so quite other that, in comparison, marrying Miss Gostrey would be
almost of the old order.[15]

This passage may superficially admit of the interpretation that it is
Strether's American asceticism that stands in his way. However, this
does not take his "total little experience" into account. What really
obstructs him—and wouldn't have done so earlier, as James notes—is his
final awareness that either way of life is insufficient tribute to Life. To
marry Miss Gostrey would not in itself destroy his independence, but
it would be a symbolic avowal that her world, the European one, corresponds to what he wants.[16] Europe comes closer than America, perhaps, but both fall so far short of the ideal that Strether prefers to forego
them both. Like Hyacinth's suicide, this is a gesture of affirmation at
the same time that it is the only choice he can make, considering the
strength and nature of his vision. Strether is more heroic than Hyacinth,
because his sacrifice is not demanded by a physical threat. His return
to a life that can hold few pleasures, no comfortable illusions, no
righteous prejudices, little in short except a continuous stream of insult to his widened consciousness, is his supreme tribute to Life as a
whole. Marrying Miss Gostrey would have committed him to a manner of living which, a few weeks before, he felt perfectly prepared to
enjoy, and to which he could still easily habituate himself. But this
would be false to his vision. Strether has indeed emerged, as James says,
"on the other side" of his social adventure. His final renunciation, so
subtly couched in a refusal to hide from Woollett, is the perfect, necessary conclusion to the gradual extension of his awareness. Again we
arrive at the supreme Jamesian irony, that a full appreciation of Life
is incompatible with the everyday business of living. Strether, like
Hyacinth, refuses to save himself from the war of his two societies.
His vision is worth its price.

15. *Notebooks*, p. 415.
16. James confessed to Grace Norton: "One's attitude toward marriage is . . . the most
characteristic part doubtless of one's general attitude toward life . . . If I were to marry
I should be guilty in my own eyes of inconsistency—I should pretend to think quite a
little better of life than I really do." Quoted by F. O. Matthiessen, *Henry James: the Major
Phase* (New York, Oxford University Press, 1944), p. 50.

CHAPTER 3

The Wings of the Dove

ALTHOUGH *The Wings of the Dove* was published one year before *The Ambassadors*, it is actually a later work. James finished *The Ambassadors* sometime around June of 1901, and must have begun *The Wings of the Dove* immediately thereafter. The germ of *The Ambassadors* was an anecdote he heard in 1895, and by 1900 he had written an elaborate outline of the book; but *The Wings of the Dove* was of much longer incubation than this. James began to shape the plot in 1894, but at least one of the central characters was adapted from *The Portrait of a Lady,* and the basis of the action had deep roots in James's personal life—deeper and older than any aspect of *The Ambassadors.* As the author states at the beginning of his preface, " 'The Wings of the Dove,' published in 1902, represents to my memory a very old—if I shouldn't perhaps rather say a very young—motive; I can scarce remember the time when the situation on which this long-drawn fiction mainly rests was not vividly present to me."[1]

This may account in part for the striking differences in style between *The Ambassadors* and *The Wings of the Dove;* in the latter novel James was so familiar with his theme that he could deal with it almost entirely by indirection, by the contrast of symbols. Although *The Ambassadors, The Wings of the Dove,* and *The Golden Bowl* are usually taken together as representative of the later style, *The Ambassadors* only begins to suggest the resources of language that James employed in the two following novels. Method and meaning, which worked hand in glove in *The Ambassadors,* are often indistinguishable in *The Wings of the Dove.* The way things were said was important enough in *The Ambassadors,* but here things sometimes *are* the way they are said. Characters and ideas simply do not exist for us apart from the images used to describe them. James's characters now conceive of everything —including each other—in terms of elaborate poetic analogies, and it

1. *The Art of the Novel,* p. 288.

gradually dawns on the reader that these analogies are all he really knows about any given character. Whereas in the earlier novels (*The Ambassadors* not excepted) the characters talked about events, here the events are often impossible to distinguish from the talk.

It will be seen that James had good dramatic reasons for this step toward abstraction, but regardless of his other motives it is certain that he saw the theme and central heroine of *The Wings of the Dove* as especially susceptible to such a treatment. "The idea, reduced to its essence," he wrote in the preface, "is that of a young person conscious of a great capacity for life, but early stricken and doomed, condemned to die under short respite, while also enamoured of the world; aware moreover of the condemnation and passionately desiring to 'put in' before extinction as many of the finer vibrations as possible, and so achieve, however briefly and brokenly, the sense of having lived."[2] This is Milly Theale in the novel, but her prototype was Minny Temple, James's cousin. William and Henry James were both stunned when she died of tuberculosis in 1871; they called the event the end of their youth. The poignancy of Minny's fate—her love of life and her inability to stay alive—remained fixed in Henry's mind, and was further romanticized by his literary imagination. Even in her lifetime Minny had seemed to be merely the suggestion of a human being. In James's eyes she was so thoroughly buried by her sense of wasted opportunity that she had no distinguishable outlines at all. When he took her as a model for Isabel Archer in 1880–81, he felt her curious vagueness as an artistic drawback. He confided to Grace Norton: "Poor Minny was essentially incomplete—and I have attempted to make my young woman [Isabel] more rounded, more finished."[3] However, by the time of *The Wings of the Dove* James was interested in roundness of a different sort, and now he saw Minny's indefiniteness as a positive advantage. In Milly Theale she became an indistinct, powerful symbol for life and loss, for beauty and the annihilation of beauty, and James deliberately refrained from "bringing her to life" in terms of everyday facts.[4]

James's notebooks make it clear that Milly's plight was the moral center of the novel and the first source of his interest. We even know,

2. *Ibid.*

3. Quoted by Matthiessen, *The Major Phase*, p. 49.

4. Those who are annoyed by this will find comfort in F. R. Leavis, *The Great Tradition* (New York, Doubleday, 1954), p. 193. Leavis finds Milly indefinite to the point of nonexistence, and is thoroughly disgruntled.

from a comparison of two successive entries in 1894, that he invented
Kate Croy only as a foil, first passive and then positively evil, for
Milly's pervasive innocence. However, this should not be emphasized
too heavily. Kate Croy and her fiancé Merton Densher, once created,
are just as involved in the novel's meaning as Milly is. Indeed, as real
people whose actions are understandable in terms of normal human
aspirations, they play a more complicated role than Milly herself. Even
when exerting her power, Milly is somehow passive and intangible;
her status as a symbol always prevails. But Kate and Merton belong to
a more palpable world, and most of the novel's action is reflected in
the lively eye of one or the other of them. Together they are extraordinarily aware of Milly's spirituality, but are themselves much more
mundane. In fact, James has been criticized for confusing the two
worlds in his imagery.[5] Some critics feel that Kate and Merton, as
people who know what they want and proceed systematically to get
it, seem all too sensitive to Milly's vague soulfulness.

However, to take this attitude is to misunderstand an extremely
useful refinement of technique. Kate and Densher, and even Kate's
vulgarly acquisitive aunt Maud, are all sensitive to Milly's tragedy, and
they all sympathize with her; but this does not preclude their exploiting
her, any more than it would in real life. In purifying the motives of his
characters James has reached a stage at which personal enmity is not only
unnecessary to evil-doing, it is regarded as an element of moral re-
dundancy. If "natural enemies" in material ambition are placed in
genuine sympathy with one another, we may take the measure of their
selfishness, their true immorality, by weighing it against the opposite
pull of friendship. Thus genuine villainy can no longer be confused
with petty resentment. Kate "uses" Milly *in spite of* her admiration for
her, and although the battle of conscience in Kate's mind is never seen
as clearly as in Densher's, it adds to the richness of suggested meaning.

Of course it is difficult to say how real such affection as Kate's for
Milly is; James can use the language of high flattery with bitterly
ironical intent, as we shall see. In his notes of November 7, 1894, he
wrote that the two girls "*must not love each other.*"[6] However, this
necessity, even if we assume that James still thought it valid in 1901,
does not exclude the various degrees of attraction between indifference

5. See, e.g., Stephen Spender, *The Destructive Element* (London, Jonathan Cape, 1935),
pp. 73f.
6. *Notebooks*, p. 172.

and love. Kate certainly doesn't love Milly, if indeed she likes her personally at all. But she *admires* her, just as everyone else except Densher admires her.[7] This admiration seems to derive partly from a perception of the social uniqueness of Milly's position, and partly from sheer romantic sentimentality. Milly's plight, which I shall discuss in more detail later, is nothing short of soap-operatic, and her visible response to it, the social role she makes of it, is played on a grand scale. She is the stricken but stoical princess. Kate and Maud and especially Susan Stringham, Milly's traveling companion, deal with her on these exaggerated terms; her moral stature impresses them only in its social manifestation. The paradox of great material wealth coupled with utter homelessness is of great interest to people who know that social intercourse is largely a matter of accepted gestures. Milly accepts nothing. She forges her way through London society on the sole basis of her personal charm—a charm made possible by money, but nonetheless a genuine one. Kate and Maud do not ask themselves whether the charm or the money is uppermost in their admiration for her, and it is only in retrospect that we can make this distinction ourselves. James is careful to circumvent any occasion for a frank analysis of motives. The situation is arranged so that "what's good for Milly" at any given moment also seems to be good for the other characters, with the consequence that the rightness or wrongness of any act can no longer be inferred from its good or bad effects. Some of the most selfish deeds appear to produce satisfactory results for all concerned.

Thus "good manners" sustain a pressing ambiguity in the all-important question of what the major characters think of each other. Surfaces and depths are so far from interchangeable that we must read every profession of good will with a readiness to find multiple hypocrisies in it. All the characters do their best, socially, for the others, and personal resentment is all but invisible in the general fog of benevolence. To judge any deed we must go back to its very nature. Was it motivated by greed or by generosity? Did it serve the interests of the other characters by design, or by mere coincidence with one's own interest? Although ambiguity is never altogether dispelled, the final attitude of the moral hero provides an approximate answer. But in

7. It is significant that while Merton Densher is the only character to arrive at a full appreciation of Milly, he is also the only one who is unimpressed by her at first sight. In retrospect we might take this as a preliminary hint that the others are admiring something less than "the real Milly."

this novel the moral hero emerges only in the last pages of the book, and for most of the time we must be content merely to collect evidence and suspend our judgment.

This type of subtlety has condemned James to a wide variety of interpretations. Some readers, perceiving the significant fact that good manners can be used to disguise the shabbiest motives, tend to deny that the scheming characters are at all capable of moral feeling. Others draw the opposite conclusion; they say that the mutual friendship of James's later characters proves that there are no real "villains" in these novels. This leads to moral generalizations quite different from my own. Stephen Spender, the most cogent spokesman for this view, reaches the following decision: "Once the situation is provided the actors cannot behave otherwise. Their only compensation is that by the use of their intelligence, by their ability to understand, to love, and to suffer, they may to some extent atone for the evil which is simply the evil of their modern world. It is these considerations that make his later books parables of modern Western civilization."[8] Spender assumes that the individual is innocent and helpless, and that his particular dilemma corrupts his action, through his "unconscious," without really corrupting his soul. No one is guilty but society itself, which demands incompatible types of feeling from the individual. In short, man is good but his world is bad.

Spender's view cannot be entirely disregarded in any interpretation of James. It is quite true that Kate's inordinate desire for money is a symptom of modern society's tendency to divorce wealth from culture; Hyacinth and Strether suffered from the same predicament. Kate is not greedy in the abstract, but is motivated by a deep, almost instinctive desire to escape her "modern" dilemma. And yet Spender seems to have upset one of James's careful balances of emphasis by putting too much weight on one factor. Granted that Kate's predicament is an unpleasant one, who forces her to solve it by exploiting Milly? Modern society may be evil (although this in itself is a half-truth) without being held responsible for the sins of its individual members. Some characters, like Hyacinth, are perfectly able to suffer from social injustice without becoming unjust themselves. Kate's "ability to understand, to love, and to suffer" does not keep her from persisting in a completely heartless course of action, in the face of a moral beauty that strikes Merton Den-

8. *The Destructive Element*, p. 67.

sher so deeply that he finds himself quite able to "behave otherwise" at the end. Indeed, what he finally rejects is precisely Spender's deterministic view of the matter. He comes to understand that by obeying his moral insight at the start, or even in the middle of the affair, he could have saved Milly from betrayal. I make this point now because in Spender's reading of James it is virtually irrelevant to ask which characters are morally superior to the others. My own feeling is that this issue is of the first importance, and must occupy the greater part of our attention. We can say, flatly, that every character in *The Wings of the Dove* is a product of his society, and is therefore to a certain extent innocent of his own thoughts. But having said so, we ought to look further and see whether James may not be implying that some characters, after all, are not so innocent as others.

The character whose innocence is most in question is Kate Croy, and James took great trouble to portray her features and circumstances roundly. Indeed, he let the task occupy him so thoroughly that the first two books grew to a disturbing length, compelling him to foreshorten many later scenes. In using Lionel Croy, Marian Condrip, and the sisters Condrip to "explain" Kate, James had to develop these characters in more detail than their usefulness to the rest of the action merited. But the immediate goal was achieved. Kate's sordid background becomes so real that we see Kate herself as markedly, heroically superior to it. She exemplifies what R. P. Blackmur calls James's concept of intelligence, namely "taste in action."[9] She has "stature without height, grace without motion, presence without mass."[10] That is to say, she has the social virtues that Chad learned from Madame de Vionnet. In addition to this she is tremendously courageous, ambitious, and proud. Involved in a financial and ethical disgrace incurred by her father and shared by her elder sister Marian, Kate exhibits none of their pettiness and defeatism. "Personally, at least, she was not chalk-marked for the auction." (*1, 6*) It is only through a conscious effort that she avoids lapsing into the frank acquisitiveness we recognize in Marian, or the self-pitying bitterness of her father. It is, to be more precise, her sense of personal and family honor that saves her.

But Kate is no less concerned with money than her relatives are. If

9. R. P. Blackmur, "Henry James," *Literary History of the United States,* eds. Robert Spiller et al. (New York, Macmillan, 1948), *2,* 1057.

10. Henry James, *The Wings of the Dove* (2 vols. in one, New York, Modern Library, 1946), *1,* 5f.

anything she sees the necessity of financial improvement more keenly than the others, for she is the one who is most aware of the social and cultural value of money. She is painfully conscious of being the sort of person who cannot thrive without material luxuries; she has "a dire accessibility to pleasure from such sources." (*1,* 31) As a result she is intensely practical and hardheaded, despite a residue of romantic feeling. She has "seen the general show too early and too sharply" (*1,* 73) to be able to accept things as they come. She must make her own luck.

With this fact made abundantly clear in the first two books, the reader may question how anyone can doubt the selfishness of Kate's motives in the forthcoming crisis. But in James's actual presentation she is seen as a complex, almost self-contradictory person. Her good taste is played off against her ambition as well as against the poor taste of her family, so that we really don't see which is stronger in her, ambition or taste. Getting hold of a dying orphan's money has, after all, an odor of vulgarity, and Kate is shown to be a person who will do almost anything to keep from being vulgar—this in fact is why she needs money in the first place. To demonstrate her stress on taste James presents her with a simple option between accepting Maud Lowder's rich but bloated hospitality and living in simple poverty with her dishonored father. Although Lionel Croy himself rules out the latter possibility, we learn at least that this was Kate's own preference. We therefore know that she has turned herself over to Aunt Maud only in desperation.

The matter of taste is also central in Kate's relationship with the penniless Merton Densher. "He represented what her life had never given her and certainly, without some such aid as his, never would give her; all the high, dim things she lumped together as of the mind." (*1,* 57) This is extremely important in our judgment of Kate, for it shows her as "expansive" in somewhat the same way that James's most sympathetic heroes are. She doesn't simply want to acquire and collect things, she wants to broaden her capacity for understanding. Money, again, is a means toward this end, but her association with Densher is an even more direct means to it. The fact that she stands by Densher before he has any hopes of becoming wealthy should prove to the reader that she does not want money for its own sake. If her sense of self-interest is unwavering, it is self-interest conceived on an exalted plane. By the time that Milly Theale arrives in London Kate has shown herself a woman of considerable scrupulousness, and we can have no clear idea of whether she sees Milly as an object of pity and admiration or as a potential victim of her own superior acuteness.

The picture we get of Maud Lowder is less ambiguous. Kate thinks of her as "Britannia of the Market Place" (*1, 34*), and Lionel Croy bluntly names her an "elephantine snob" (*1, 21*). She is a personification of vulgar middle-class ambition. Her whole world is epitomized in the objects that adorn her home at Lancaster Gate, and through Densher's eyes these "fringed and scalloped" monstrosities, reminiscent of Water-bath in *The Spoils of Poynton,* take on a moral value: "But it was, above all, the solid forms, the wasted finish, the misguided cost, the general attestation of morality and money, a good conscience and a big balance. These things finally represented for him a portentous negation of his own world of thought . . ." (*1, 88*) Kate regards her as all "personality," dangerously assertive and possessive: "It was perfectly present to Kate that she might be devoured, and she likened herself to a trembling kid, kept apart a day or two till her turn should come, but sure sooner or later to be introduced into the cage of the lioness." (*1, 33*) As for her place in James's catalogue of intensely empty and bloatedly full char-acters—a pattern of imagery which applies no less tellingly here than in *The Ambassadors*—the following passage should suffice to fix her: "Mrs. Lowder . . . was spacious because she was full, because she had something in common, even in repose, with a projectile, of great size, loaded and ready for use." (*1, 187*)

If Maud's presence is gross, her methods are, like a projectile's, sleek and efficient. Like many of James's cunning plotters, including Kate herself, she knows that the minimum course is not simply the most discreet but usually the most effective one as well. She is so sure of her power that she doesn't have to exercise it; her leniency seems almost like generosity. This circumspection is especially evident in her handl-ing of Kate and Merton, whose romance is objectionable to her on the grounds of Densher's poverty. She gives the lovers exactly as much freedom as they think it wise to employ—that quantity having been diminished by their fear of her wrath and their indebtedness to her liberality. She knows, or thinks she knows, exactly how magnanimous she can afford to be. Thus Densher imagines her as conveying the fol-lowing message to him: "Do you suppose me so stupid as to quarrel with you if it's not really necessary? It won't—it would be too absurd! —*be* necessary. I can bite your head off any day, any day I really open my mouth; and I'm dealing with you now, see—and successfully judge—without opening it. I do things handsomely all round—I place you in the presence of the plan with which, from the moment it's a case of taking you seriously, you're incompatible." (1, 94) This is of course not magnanimity but a further infatuation with power. In this affair Maud is doing her best to consider herself a member of the leisure class.

However, her treatment of Densher is complicated by the fact that she herself is attracted to him. For a while she thinks she understands him even better than Kate does, and she is influenced by a desire to keep him available to her household. As Densher explains to Kate, this feeling is not inconsistent with Maud's acquisitiveness: "She doesn't disparage intellect and culture—quite the contrary; she wants them to adorn her board and be named in her programme." (1, 99) There is a real conflict in her mind between Densher's positive ornamental value and his dangerousness as Kate's suitor. In her own powerful and narrow-minded way Maud has a streak of generosity: "she could almost at any hour, by a kindled preference or a diverted energy, glow for another interest than her own." (1, 295) Even her desire to have Kate marry richly, despite all the project's value as a test of her "buying power," must be seen at least partially as evidence of good will toward Kate. She is so dominated in her thinking by the apparent identity of wealth and happiness that she can be said to be genuinely considering Kate's happiness when she insists that Kate become wealthy.

If we contrast this view with the more sophisticated and enlightened attitude of Kate herself, we are forced to think of Aunt Maud as a naïve bungler. Kate is two steps ahead of her all the way through the novel. In fact, Maud never even arrives at a comprehension of Kate's basic plan for exploiting Milly. Her Achilles heel is her faith in the financial basis of Kate's pride. She knows how devoted to "improvement" her niece is, and how little a match with Densher could mitigate the dishonor of her family—a dishonor that she herself avoids by refusing to consider Lionel Croy and the Condrips as relatives. Social honor can be bought, as Kate and Maud are both aware. Once having assumed that honor is the most important thing in Kate's life, Maud cannot imagine that she would consider Densher seriously as a husband. She does not realize at first that Kate has an emotional as well as a practical side, and that her sense of honor is not translatable into pounds and shillings. Kate will not settle for money alone. Instead of choosing between Densher's love and Maud's fortune, she sets to work to keep both of them.

The most innocent figure in this intrigue is Merton Densher himself, an out-and-out intellectual who has no pretensions to worldliness. By virtue of his youth and his miscellaneous education he is a formless, and hence socially harmless, young man: "He suggested above all . . . that wondrous state of youth in which the elements, the metals more or less precious, are so in fusion and fermentation that the question of the final stamp, the pressure that fixes the value, must wait for comparative coolness." (*1, 55*) While Kate's strength is all for the business of getting and spending, Densher's is all for abstract thought. But he has a "weakness for life," if not an aptitude for it, just as, on the opposite side, Kate has a weakness but no talent for things "of the mind." They seem perfectly suited, each fulfilling the other's most deeply felt shortcomings.

The most important element in Densher's character is what James calls his "straightness," a quality that becomes increasingly central to the novel's meaning in the closing books. We are told almost in so many words that this moral asset stems from Densher's never having adjusted himself to English society, although the cause of his discomfort is left unspecified: "But brave enough though his descent to English earth, he had passed, by the way, through zones of air that had left their ruffle on his wings, had been exposed to initiations ineffaceable. Something had happened to him that could never be undone." (*1, 104*) Outwardly he is an earnest, intelligent young journalist with a moderately successful career ahead of him, but for the reader he comes to assume the role of an oracle for James's own opinions. Like Strether, he tries to stand intellectually outside the action of his novel. When he finally realizes that he is very much involved in it he takes positive action of his own, and this action, as we might expect, is our best clue to the author's moral judgment of his principal characters.

Book III introduces the most romantic and ethereal heroine in all Jamesian fiction. Milly Theale is fabulously rich, touchingly inexperienced, totally bereft of relatives, and is dying of an unnamed disease. James does not blush to say that his heroine's state is thoroughly poignant, even without the consideration of her imminent death. Milly's fate is to combine a sense of limitless possibility with an equally strong sense of unfulfillment. To have every material advantage, "and then on top of all to enjoy boundless freedom, the freedom of the wind in the desert—it was unspeakably touching to be so equipped and yet to have been reduced by fortune to little humble-minded mistakes." (*1*, 123) This impression is recorded in the sentimental brain of Milly's traveling companion, Susan Stringham, and as such it can be taken with a grain of salt. But I think James himself saw Milly as "unspeakably touching," and meant the reader to see her that way. He deliberately emphasizes the enormous scope of her tragedy, "explaining" it in semimythical terms which make it all the more grandiose:

It was New York mourning, it was New York hair, it was a New York history . . . of the loss of parents, brothers, sisters, almost every human appendage, all on a scale and with a sweep that had required the greater stage; it was a New York legend of affecting, of romantic isolation, and, beyond everything, it was by most accounts, in respect to the mass of money so piled on the girl's back, a set of New York possibilities. [*1*, 118]

Although New York thus conduces to a romantic consciousness, it provides no outlet for it; it cannot save the heroine from "little humble-minded mistakes." Only in Europe, where no native is concerned to acquire a sense of romance, can the American soul find a rich enough climate in which to thrive. Milly's trip to Europe is designed to be the only "fling" of her shattered career; it represents for her a single, brief panorama of Life in the broadest sense—the only sense she is equipped to understand.

As Susan remarks, Milly is "starved for culture," and like Hyacinth and Strether she goes through a process of social education. Susan, whose Boston hat symbolizes the extent to which she is a woman of the world—"so Tyrolese, yet somehow, though feathered from the eagle's wing, so truly domestic" (*1*, 120f.)—at first seems to Milly to embody all the assembled heritage of human civilization. When Milly arrives in England and meets Kate and Maud her world becomes suddenly bigger, so much so that at first she mistakes her new vision for "the real thing." The point at which she becomes disenchanted with this illusion is not precisely fixed, although we can infer from the book's catastrophe that she has never achieved a dispassionate, realistic view of society. It is important to remember that from her arrival in London until she renounces life altogether, Milly will be at the social mercy of Kate and Maud. In contrast to our earlier heroes, she seems incapable of profiting from her worldly experience.

Having an abundance of money, she can afford not to think of finance at all. She literally ignores it, in marked contrast to the only other wealthy character in the novel: "Aunt Maud sat somehow in the midst of her money, founded on it and surrounded by it, even if with a clever high manner about it, her manner of looking, hard and bright, as if it weren't there. Milly, about hers, had no manner at all . . . she was at any rate far away on the edge of it, and you hadn't, as might be said, in order to get at her nature, to traverse . . . any piece of her property." (1, 216) Still, she cannot escape the fact of her wealth. Her every gesture and appurtenance, however casual, bears the stamp of a millionairess. "She couldn't have lost it if she had tried—that was what it was to be really rich." (1, 136) That she does in a sense want to lose her money implies not only a knowledge that she will never have time to "spend" it, i.e. to assume and enjoy a social position, but also a desire to eliminate the barriers between herself and other people. She wants to understand and to love the things she will meet, not to buy them. She must deal with them disinterestedly if she is to comprehend them for what they are.

This brings me to what I consider to be Milly's real tragedy, apart from the obvious and overstated theme of wasted opportunity. Milly's tragedy is that she cannot escape the romantic appeal of her situation. When I said earlier that the other characters admire her, I meant that they sympathize with her melodramatic plight. The greatest source of Milly's frustration is just this sympathy. It creates a wall of pity between herself and others. She tries desperately to "normalize" herself, to make people behave naturally with her: "She literally felt . . . that her only company must be the human race at large, present all round her, but inspiringly impersonal . . ." (1, 270) But she is doomed to be regarded as a fairy princess, and in spite of herself she contributes to this attitude by showing a full awareness of her special circumstances. Eventually she abandons her attempt at "realism" and plays her imposed part grandly, hoping to find love (for lack of love may be called her disease) by frankly cultivating the social impressiveness of her position. But this takes effect too late to save her, and she dies with only one bitter taste of the emotional truth she came to Europe to find.

Nevertheless, Milly does become superficially acquainted with a civilization unknown to New York, and she is fascinated by it. For both Susan and herself English society is a "labyrinth," and she regards the study of its complex workings as "fun." The social intrigue that most interests her is that between Kate, Densher, and Maud, and the reason for her special interest is a private one: she herself has fallen in love with Densher, whom she met in America a few months earlier. But Milly is so awed by Kate that she abandons her hopes for Densher as soon as she becomes convinced that Kate loves him. Kate represents a phenomenon so refreshing, so exotic in Milly's proper little world that she can see Kate's shortcomings almost as virtues: "the handsome girl was, with twenty other splendid qualities, the least bit brutal too, and didn't she suggest, as no one yet had ever done for her new friend, that there might be a wild beauty in that, and even a strange grace?" (1, 201) This typifies her reaction to English society as a whole. She sees it as deep, mysterious, and vicious, but also as "fun." Inasmuch as it corresponds to no values with which she is familiar, she is unequipped to regard it as positively evil. Besides, she has come too far to lapse into moralism; she simply wants to distinguish reality from sham. "I want abysses," (1, 206) she tells her Boston confidante. Having found them, or thinking so, she does not want to reject them as immoral.

Kate Croy gladly fosters this attitude by proposing to Milly a genial, amoral philosophy of human relations: "every one who had anything to give . . . made the sharpest possible bargain for it, got at least its value in return. The strangest thing, furthermore, was that this might be, in cases, a happy understanding. The worker in one connection was the worked in another; it was as broad as it was long—with the wheels of the system, as might be seen, wonderfully oiled. People could quite like each other in the midst of it . . ." (1, 198) Such explanations may be taken as evidence of a moral uneasiness in Kate's mind, a need for self-justification. She speaks in order to "educate" Milly, but "quite conceivably for her own relief as well." (1, 302) As she comes increasingly to feel the cruelty of her scheme, she places more and more of the responsibility for evil on society in the abstract. Soon the machine has become a monster: "It might, the monster, Kate conceded, loom large for those born amid forms less developed and therefore no doubt less amusing; it might on some sides be a strange and dreadful monster, calculated to devour the unwary, to abase the proud, to scandalise the good . . ." (1, 302f.) Milly accepts this view without hesitation, but it has no influence on her idealistic sense of truth. She cannot draw the connection between Kate's nervous confessions and the actual "monstrosity" of Kate's attitude toward herself. Thus she conceives of social intrigue as a harmless game, a make-believe, rather than as a morally serious business. She "had amusements of thought that were like the secrecies of a little girl playing with dolls when conventionally 'too big.' " (*1*, 233) Her observation is sometimes acute, but she is dangerously, vulnerably naïve.

Her naïveté is fostered by the circumstance, already noted, of everyone's interests seeming to point to the same goals. Kate's general plan is to allow Milly's love for Densher to ripen until, with or without marriage, Milly turns over her money to him. Even if Milly were capable of perceiving such a bold plot, she wouldn't have to see its true motivation: Kate could just as plausibly be "lending" her fiancé to the dying girl out of pity. Densher's motive could be construed as the same. As for Aunt Maud, Densher's interest in Milly suits her perfectly, both as a boon to Milly and, more profitably, as a means of keeping Densher away from Kate. Milly, in spite of her love of truth, cannot resist taking the most romantic and generous course in her judgments of people. She calls Maud "an idealist" (*1*, 178), and thinks of Kate's dissimulations as "a sort of failure of common terms" (*1*, 210) between Kate and herself. She can even equate the English "awfully good manner" with "the conscious sinking of a consciousness" (*1*, 211) without perceiving that this fact poses a danger to herself. Although she is usually able to see what other people want, she finds no reason to ask *why* they want it.

In her sentimental haze Milly lumps together things that she should have kept separate for her own protection. Not the least of these is her association of Matcham, the ambitious Lord Mark's estate, with her special tragedy. She allows Lord Mark to see that she has been moved by the somber, ancient air of the place, and in particular by a Bronzino portrait of a girl who resembles herself. Seeing the liveliness of the portrait and then recalling that its subject must now be dead, Milly is reminded of her own impending death. This in turn momentarily strengthens her belief that Lord Mark, as he professes, simply wants to "take care of you a little." (*1*, 241) Lord Mark's beneficence is not so apparent to the reader; we are led to suspect that he wants to take care only of Milly's money, as Kate and Densher finally agree. But he too is an ambiguous figure. He is the penniless modern nobleman, full of inherited charm and devoid of inherited means. As Milly tells him frankly, he is blasé without being really enlightened. Yet he appears to be genuinely attracted to Milly, and his rash behavior at the end of the book can be interpreted as the jealousy of a disappointed lover. In any case, Milly never seriously doubts the kindness of his intentions. She recognizes that he has been "working Lancaster Gate for all it was worth" (*1, 197*), but she has not yet learned that more than one scheme can be worked at a time. Through her unwariness she gives Lord Mark just enough accidental encouragement for him to entertain hopes which eventually lead to disaster.

As Kate's scheme gradually becomes clear to Densher, relations between them become strained. Densher does not relish the idea of deceiving Milly for her fortune, and he is surprised that Kate is able to suppress her conscience so effectively. But at the proper moment Kate plays her best card: she mentions that Milly would be far more injured by Densher's *not* courting her. He eventually sees that, given Milly's attraction to him, failure would have "an appearance of barbarity." (*2, 79*) The larger question of whether Kate has deliberately fostered this attraction is never considered. Like Milly, Densher will not face the issue until things begin to go wrong, and if Milly looms at this point as "an angel with a thumping bank-account" (*2, 57*), so much the better for all concerned. Kate's plan also has the advantage of throwing Aunt Maud off her guard about Densher's relations with her niece; it is generally agreed that any false dealing with Maud is justified by that lady's own policies and intentions.

Densher's "straightness" does begin to appear fairly early, however, if only in the form of insulted masculinity. With the exception of Lord Mark and the almost mystical doctor, Luke Strett, whose intuitiveness places him rather with the female characters than the male, Densher is entirely surrounded by women—all of whom, including Milly, are neck deep in subtleties. This has made him uneasy from the beginning, but the strain becomes much greater when he sees that Kate will not object to his marrying another woman. His one force for patience, the assurance that Kate loves him, is drastically weakened. How can she see him turned over to Milly without so much as seeming to find it awkward? In his anguish Densher asks himself only whether or not Kate really loves him; he should ask, rather, to what degree Kate is willing to subdue her affections and her conscience for the sake of money. It is perfectly obvious that she loves him, and she strikes me as getting off easily, even at the expense of her chastity, in being asked only to prove that love. The real moral issue is deferred and distorted by means of a sexual appeal to Densher's masculine pride. He states very neatly his awareness of the moral crudity in their plan when he proposes to Kate, as a simple business transaction, "I'll tell any lie you want, any your idea requires, if you'll only come to me." (2, 219)

By this point the intrigue is running fully under its own power, and the scene has been changed to Venice for the climactic developments. Milly, fully resigned to her role as fairy princess, rents a palazzo and all the trimmings, with a suave and extravagant manager, Eugenio, to handle the details: "he was forever carrying one well-kept Italian hand to his heart and plunging the other straight into her pocket . . ." (2, 146) The principal characters gather in Milly's palace, which becomes at once a symbol of her unreal world and a stage for her battle to survive: "The romance for her . . . would be to sit there forever, through all her time, as in a fortress; and the idea became an image of never going down, of remaining aloft in the divine, dustless air, where she would hear but the plash of the water against stone." (2, 162) This passage is meaningful in the light of image patterns that have been accumulating throughout the novel. Water has generally been associated with the social medium, the fluid upon which the characters maneuver, pass each other, and occasionally collide. Images of the overflowing of water, while not perfectly consistent, have usually indicated a submersion of the individual in his social world, either with or without the added implication of disaster. To be surrounded by water and yet to be in a stone palace rather than a boat, and to fear submersion, is for Milly an exact metaphorical reflection of her case. She is not really a navigator in society but a lighthouse keeper; she combines the enjoyment of "hearing the water" with that of breathing a "divine, dustless air." But when all is said and done she is fated to sink into the water like everyone else. The situation is stressed again and again: "She was *in* it [the palace], as in the ark of her deluge, and filled with such a tenderness for it that why shouldn't this, in common mercy, be warrant enough? She would never, never leave it . . . would ask nothing more than to sit tight in it and float on and on." (2, 157) This passive floating is much different from the energetic paddling and turning that has been ascribed to Maud and Kate. The fact that Milly does expire in Venice, after we have been subjected to a long series of images connecting water with society, supports the inference Densher finally makes, that social intrigue has been the cause of her death.

The Wings of the Dove begins in a tone of sardonic irony, in dealing with the tough, practical world from which Kate is struggling to escape. The middle section of the book, where Kate and Milly are brought into contrast, is handled more metaphorically. In Venice, as

Milly appears gradually more impressive as a suffering princess, the style becomes correspondingly more figurative, until at the end we are reading what amounts to lyrical poetry. The romantic images that surround Milly, and which were occasionally depreciated earlier by the fact that they were linked with hypocritical or unduly sentimental thoughts, now occupy the center of the stage. Milly's spiritual inviolability by earthly things is increasingly stressed, and her moral victory will be complete when her full allegorical value has been accepted by the other characters.

This acceptance is complicated by the fact that some of the characters have been paying lip service to Milly's value all along. Susan's conception of her as a princess has been generally and cordially accepted, and Kate had told her she was "a dove" as early as Book v (*1*, 308).[11] The dove image has even been applied to Maud Lowder (*1*, 310), who is otherwise connected to a more dangerous set of figures (lion, eagle, bomb). The only principal character who hasn't cheapened Milly's iconography through glibness is Densher, the "straight" one. Now, in the final books, Densher's evaluation of Milly becomes the moral heart of the novel. Hitherto she has been simply "little Miss Theale from New York," but now her very frankness, her unpretentious friendliness, begins to impress him as a virtue. "It made her unity and was the one thing he could unlimitedly take for granted in her." (*2*, 278f.) When he contrasts this openness with his own duplicity he sees a tremendous strength of innocence in Milly's character: "He then fairly perceived that—even putting their purity of motive at its highest —it was neither Kate nor he who made his strange relation to Milly, who made her own, so far as it might be, innocent . . . Milly herself did everything . . ." (*2*, 261) Although he has not yet realized the selfishness of Kate's plan, and is still in love with her, Densher has at least seen that part of Milly's radiance is genuine. It remains for him to recognize that the palace and the manner of a princess are only reflections of an inner beauty. Milly is touching not simply because of her poignant situation, but because she is spiritually *good*. This is the conclusion Densher is gradually encouraged to draw.

The difference between his behavior toward Kate and toward Milly

11. This is the first of many dove images, and it comes at a significant point: a few lines earlier Milly had thought to herself that Kate "paced like a panther." The contrast of innocence and nervous aggressiveness in the pairing of the two images is striking and surely deliberate.

is a clue to the relative inferiority of Kate's ultimate spiritual appeal. What he calls his "feelings" "were all for Kate, without a feather's weight to spare." (2, 223) For the personal facts of Milly's case "he hadn't even the amount of curiosity that he would have had about an ordinary friend." (2, 223) But in spite of this Kate tells him plainly that he is in love with Milly. She says it at first apparently to test his reaction, but when she repeats her statement at the end of the novel it is because she has seen that it is true. As James planned in his notebook, Densher has fallen in love with the spiritual beauty that Milly represents. He has perceived that she is morally uncompromised by any special interest, and in Densher's eyes this is a remarkable, almost a supernatural, condition. In comparison Kate seems harshly materialistic. The ambiguous dove symbol is used at a crucial moment to bring out this contrast. Kate has just remarked how Milly's jewels seem to enhance her dovelike qualities: "Milly was indeed a dove; this was the figure, though it most applied to her spirit. But he knew in a moment that Kate was just now, for reasons hidden from him, exceptionally under the impression of that element of wealth in her . . . which was dove-like only so far as one remembered that doves have wings and wondrous flights . . ." (2, 238) As the scene progresses, Densher becomes more fully aware of Kate's need for money and of his own present inability to supply it; this refastens him to his unpleasant task. But in the meantime he has made a highly disturbing comparison between his own new way of conceiving Milly—the only way that does proper justice to her—and, on the other hand, Kate's practical view of her as a potential source of income. Kate is not interested in the dove itself so much as she is in where it is going to land.

Densher is henceforth increasingly aware of Kate's shortcomings, and these can no longer be obscured through an appeal to direct physical love; Kate has returned to England with Maud. He views the whole affair more and more in the purer light that Milly emanates, until he finally realizes that, however comforting his presence may be to her, he is deeply betraying her spirit of honesty. "He was staying so little 'for' Milly that he was staying positively against her." (2, 273) This is the most important step in his slow, reluctant march to condemn Kate morally, for it is the first time he has admitted a disparity between Kate's aim and Milly's true welfare. When he has reached the stage where he is forced to agree with Eugenio's unspoken appraisal of him as a fortune hunter, he continues "courting" Milly only out of obedience to his bargain with Kate—a bargain he had proposed himself. His conscience interferes with his effort at deception so obviously that when Lord Mark, in jealous revenge, informs Milly of Kate's and Densher's engagement, Milly sees the whole picture at once, and "turns her face to the wall."

Luke Strett's prescription to Milly had been simply to "live," and she has kept herself going only on the basis of her desire to do so. For Milly, as for Hyacinth and Strether, this "living" has been conceived on an impossibly high plane. But whereas the two earlier heroes arrived at the idea only by comparing and rejecting a series of half-truths, Milly has possessed a kind of inclusiveness from the very start. Yet she has never had the capacity for genuine social contact. Somewhat like the Lady of Shalott, she is destroyed by her first direct meeting with reality. She had hoped to fasten her notions of the ideal on Densher, thereby connecting her own spiritual world with Densher's practical one. Her death is the measure of her failure. I think it is wrong to see this death as a grandly altruistic renunciation, as R. P. Blackmur does.[12] Turning one's face to the wall somehow lacks this heroic flavor, and Milly is much too stunned by her disenchantment with Densher to be thought of as rationally weighing alternatives. At the most we can say that she judges death to be the only way of preserving her defrauded, insulted good faith; but her end, like the Lady of Shalott's, is too sudden and automatic to be taken as a conscious moral decision. She is sacrificed as a martyr, but the choice of martyrdom is not her own. Matthiessen probably had something similar in mind when he remarked that Milly's suffering is fitting for a Desdemona, but not for an Othello.[13]

Matthiessen concluded that Milly's passivity and total innocence make her insufficient as a traditional tragic heroine. This seems correct, yet Matthiessen might have added that *The Wings of the Dove* does have an Othello of sorts. Merton Densher has allowed himself to be morally swindled no less than Othello was, and he too kills the naïve heroine through his involvement in a psychological intrigue which she has been too pure minded to comprehend until too late. Like Othello, Densher pays dearly for his blindness. In view of the fact that he is still

---

12. See "Henry James," *2*, 1057. I should add that I regard Mr. Blackmur as James's most sensitive and eloquent critic. His essay in the *Literary History* is the best short treatment of James that I have read.

13. *The Major Phase*, p. 79.

emotionally attached to Kate, his penance is scarcely less drastic than Othello's. With final access to both Milly's wealth and Kate's love, he throws them both away in deference to Milly's spiritual presence. Belatedly Densher achieves a minor tragic stature of his own.

In order for Densher's reaction to appear plausible, Milly's symbolic value must be inflated to almost Christlike proportions in the reader's mind. This is the rationale behind James's increasingly allegorical treatment of her. Milly at the end does suggest a supernatural degree of love for her enemies. There are even occasional hints that James meant us to link Milly with Christ Himself. In an early scene in the Alps she "was looking down on the kingdoms of the earth" (*1*, 139), much as Christ did in the desert.[14] Densher eventually sees her consciousness as "crucified" with pain (*2*, 368). The dove itself is a traditional Christian symbol for the Holy Spirit. Furthermore, and most important, Milly's posthumous beneficence to Kate and Densher irresistibly brings to mind the theme of Christ dying to redeem a sinful humanity. As Kate recognizes with awe, "She did it *for* us . . . she stretched out her wings, and it was to *that* they reached. They cover us." (*2*, 438) However, here as elsewhere the religious parallel is little more than a reminder of the size of Milly's beneficence. Kate's "*that*" refers not to love but to money, and it saves no one; in fact, if Densher is saved it is by virtue of *refusing* the gift. Nor is the parallel strengthened by the thought that Milly's check was signed and sealed before she had any cognizance of Densher's "sinfulness." In general we can say that Milly is occasionally likened to Christ, but that James has made no attempt to draw a consistent analogy between the two careers. His suggestions fall short of a complete allegorical pattern.

Spender proposes, without following it up, that Milly knows her gift will destroy the relationship between Kate and Densher. This is an overtone that James dared not emphasize if he had it in mind, for it seems to contradict the idea of Milly's pure love, and to render her

14. But there is a paramount difference which limits the value of the analogy. The sentence whose beginning I quote concludes: "and though indeed that of itself might well go to the brain, it wouldn't be with a view of renouncing them." James seems here to be purposely evoking and rejecting the comparison with Christ. No Satan is tempting Milly. On the other hand we cannot entirely escape the analogy with Christ's incarnation. Milly is standing above all kingdoms, and she appears to be subject to none of them —although, like Christ, she will eventually be martyred by one of them. At the moment that Susan Stringham finds her on the mountaintop she seems to be choosing which realm to invest with her spiritual presence.

capable of worldly jealousy. Nevertheless, we cannot ignore the bare
fact that she is impoverishing Densher rather than enriching him. Regardless of her motive, it functions in effect as revenge. But in one
sense this is consistent with the religious theme. She saves Densher *from*
this world, not within it, and thus her destruction of his worldly comfort may be seen as the practical form of her love. This is a Christian
idea: to be thrown off the wheel of Fortune, however painfully, is to
receive the merciful action of divine Providence. God's love is mani-
fested not only in creation of the good but in destruction of the corrupt as well.

We can turn to T. S. Eliot for a remarkably apt statement of the
same idea:

> The Dove descending breaks the air
> With flame of incandescent terror
> Of which the tongues declare
> The one discharge from sin and error.
> The only hope, or else despair
>   Lies in the choice of pyre or pyre—
>   To be redeemed from fire by fire.
>
> Who then devised the torment? Love.
> Love is the unfamiliar Name
> Behind the hands that wove
> The intolerable shirt of flame
> Which human power cannot remove.
>   We only live, only suspire
>   Consumed by either fire or fire.[15]

It is interesting enough that the death-dealing fighter plane should
suggest the dove image to Eliot; but the idea of the plane as an instrument of divine love is even more provoking. Eliot's point seems to be
that love works through purely mechanical destruction. The plane is
not God; neither is the shirt of Nessus. Nor, in *The Wings of the Dove*,
is Milly. One need assume no specific intention on her part in order
to agree that she has both ruined and redeemed Densher; she unwittingly provides an occasion for him to make his moral choice.
Significantly, the means to salvation is a sum of money—the very

15. T. S. Eliot, *Four Quartets* (London, Faber and Faber; New York, Harcourt, Brace,
1950), p. 42. I am indebted to Charles N. Feidelson, Jr., for pointing out the relevance
of these lines.

principle of corruption in Densher's world. Money redeems Densher from the influence of money.

> The only hope, or else despair
> Lies in the choice of pyre or pyre—
> To be redeemed from fire by fire.

If one sees that Densher rather than Milly is the character who acquires a tragic vision, he will agree that Milly's chief importance in the last three books lies in the impression she makes upon Densher. The basis for his liberation from error is the comparison James stated in his notebook in 1894: "In the light of how exquisite the dead girl was he sees how little exquisite is the living."[16] It should be repeated, however, that the Kate whom James had just conceived in 1894 was more obviously villainous than the one he finally created. The question we must ask is whether the eventual Kate is simply a refinement on the old one, more subtle but equally malign, or whether on the other hand she falls somewhere between innocence and guilt. The issue can never be entirely settled, for James preferred to leave Kate enshrouded in some of her ambiguities. However, remembering that Merton Densher has become a moral spokesman for the author, we can judge Kate by the final effect she produces on her fiancé.

In one word, that impression is sinister. Kate's attraction is as strong as ever, but Densher now sees it as a perverse, distorting influence. This passage illustrates the point: "She was once more close to him, close as she had been the day she came to him in Venice, the quickly-returning memory of which intensified and enriched the fact. He could practically deny in such conditions nothing that she said, and what she said was, with it, visibly, a fruit of that knowledge. 'We've succeeded.' She spoke with her eyes deep in his own. 'She won't have loved you for nothing.' It made him wince, but she insisted. 'And you won't have loved *me*.'" (2, 361) The dramatic ironies in this statement are multiple, but the most important thing to see is that Densher is now perfectly aware that Kate's power over him is an evil one. When Kate tosses Milly's farewell letter into the fire unopened, his impression is confirmed. It is an act of horrible jealousy. Kate sees that Milly is triumphantly *good,* and she cannot bear to compete with her for Densher's soul. Her final demand of Densher, the one condition upon which she will marry him, bears this out: "Your word of honour that you're not

16. *Notebooks,* p. 173.

in love with her memory." (2, 439) If Densher will renounce his faith in the martyred heroine he can be accepted on the old secular terms. If not, Kate knows that he will inwardly despise her own worldliness. When she herself lucidly proclaims at the end, "We shall never be again as we were!" (2, 439) she is sacrificing nothing that is not already gone.

It was mentioned earlier that in *The Wings of the Dove* it is not always possible to tell causes by their visible effects; the effects often satisfy a number of other causes as well.[17] Yet in spite of the fact that Milly loses nothing, physically, that she would not have lost without Kate's interference, we know from Densher's moral reaction that Kate has been deluding Milly for private gain. By the same token we see that he himself has been exploited by Kate. His ultimatum to her, the option between Milly's riches and himself, defines his consciousness of the fact that the two are now incompatible. Although it is Kate who speaks the phrase of renunciation, she is only making audible the final step in Densher's own thinking: she knows he will not be able to live with the money. We should not forget, either, that Kate's "sacrifice" of Densher is going to make her rich, and yet we need not take this as evidence that she prefers money to Densher. Simply, she realizes that Densher in his reformed state will not belong to her. Once beaten in her effort to have a husband and fortune together, Kate bows out with admirable gracefulness.

In fact, Kate is evil only in an extremely sensitive view—which is, nonetheless, the one James seems to be asking us to apply. As for her basic ability to face the truth, her courage, her sense of honor, her genuine love for Densher, and her unwavering taste, these are all of superior caliber. Furthermore, the reappearance of the Condrips near the end brings home to us once again how utterly out of place she would be in miserly, sordid conditions. Certainly she approaches Spender's description of the Jamesian character, in that she maintains a lucid and painful consciousness of her unpleasant intentions without feeling herself free to alter them. But Densher's awareness of her crime against Milly's innocence cannot be explained away, and the fact that Densher himself *is* capable of renunciation and repentance signifies to

17. We cannot even say who is most responsible for Milly's death. Kate, Densher, Lord Mark, Milly herself, society, or simply her disease can each be blamed. Physical responsibility becomes unimportant in a world where everyone feels the repercussions of every event; moral responsibility is all that really matters.

me that Kate, by comparison, is to be judged the guiltier of the two. Her steadiness of purpose is remarkable, almost heroic—but it is morally wrongheaded.

As for Densher, all his guilt has consisted in allowing Kate to over-rule his conscience. He expiates this guilt by replacing Kate's influence with the broad, ideal memory he has formed of Milly Theale. At the end of the book he has reached a point of vision which, if not so care-fully sought for as Hyacinth's and Strether's, is essentially similar in effect. His heroism is truly "modern," it barely makes itself known at all. He has had neither Hyacinth's naïve exuberance nor Strether's con-sistent integrity, but his contact with Milly has presented him with an image of the whole truth, and in the final, crucial moment he shows himself worthy of it. In terms of the International Theme he has en-dorsed an American attitude in preference to an English one, but such a statement means very little. What he has really perceived is that man's spirit—Milly—is superior to the social machine in which it is forced to operate, if it is to survive at all. The only completely sufficient homage to this spirit is to renounce the social machine, and this is the meaning of Densher's final gesture. In the moral world which Milly personified and which Densher now vindicates, renunciation is equiva-lent to salvation.

CHAPTER 4

The Golden Bowl

I.

FEW NOVELS resist clear analysis more stubbornly than *The Golden Bowl*. No novel in my acquaintance poses so many questions while providing so few definite answers, and none contains so many careful ambiguities of ultimate meaning. Ambiguity, indeed, could be called one of the book's major themes; all the action depends on the preservation of colossal misunderstandings among the four principal characters. "Hard facts," the real basis for the drama, never rise to the surface at all. They do come close enough for the characters and ourselves to form working hypotheses and to stumble toward general conclusions, but they are never so near that we can positively identify them, or deny the presence of other, less visible circumstances. James will place several conflicting explanations before us in equal relief, and then let the matter drop. No one is entirely sure of what has just happened, to say nothing of what will happen next.

This is an intensification of the dilemma we encountered in *The Wings of the Dove*. It differs essentially only in the fact that the bare moral truth, in addition to several prosaic facts, never emerges at all. Each of our previous novels reached a conclusion by eventually deflating some characters and ideals while exalting others, either directly or by implication. Milly, for example, "won out" over Kate in a schematic analysis of the novel. The reader made his moral judgments on the basis of his discovery that he had initially underestimated some characters and overestimated others. But no such final step seems possible in *The Golden Bowl*. No absolute, "real" point of perspective recommends itself to us. There is no Hyacinth or Strether or Densher to whom we can turn for James's own judgment of the action. The four "heroes" of *The Golden Bowl* are seen by the reader only as they are seen, alternately and in different lights, by each other, and James refuses to imply that one point of view is more valid than the others. In order to arrive conclusively at one set of moral insights we must therefore deny three other sets. James is scrupulous to divert us from such rashness. Any critic who has found one point of view completely vindicated is guilty of carelessness, for *The Golden Bowl* simply does not lend itself to the type of unilateral interpretation we have found applicable elsewhere.

How can we account for this disturbing fact? Part of the cause, certainly, is James's lifelong devotion to ambiguity for its own sake—the ice that will bear the skater's heaviest pressure. To "pack" his pages until they would "bristle" with meanings was the artistic ideal we find repeatedly invoked in his notes and prefaces. Yet he always enabled us to solve some or all of the principal questions; his moral theme could always be heard above the rest of his orchestration. A better approach to the problem might be to consider where James stood as a philosopher-artist at the time *The Golden Bowl* was written. *The Wings of the Dove* was in some respects the end of a chain of reasoning. In it he carried his theme of the sensitive hero's affirmation of "Life" at the expense of "life" to an ultimate extreme of pessimism. The visionary heroine was not only doomed to an eventual loss of contact with everyday existence, she never even sampled it. By clinging more tenaciously to her vision than any previous hero had done, she sacrificed every possibility of worldly satisfaction. As an artist—for the inclusive vision is essentially an artistic one—she told us in unmistakable terms that life and art are inimical. If the artist were perfectly faithful to his ideal of inclusiveness he would be incapable of existence, and hence incapable of art. One can perhaps live with this conviction, but he cannot possibly put it into affirmative practice. Compromise is the only realistic solution.

Another explanation, and possibly the most fruitful one, lies in a complication in James's sense of right and wrong. The fact that each of the previous novels affirmed the worth of its hero's "abysmal" conscience, more or less in defiance of "society," should not make us forget that society itself represented a kind of ideal. Hyacinth was killed as much by society's complex attractiveness as by its inadequacies. Strether affirmed the beauty of Madame de Vionnet's social virtues, and discovered the narrowness of a purely moralistic point of view. And Milly, the thoroughly "unsocialized" heroine, pined away for the more tangible, worldly existence that was denied her. Each hero uncovered social treacheries, but each accepted the desirability of certain social graces. In fact, the social graces came close to merging with the larger moral outlook. To observe decorum is tacitly, although often hypocritically, to admit that others are worthy of one's consideration, and this admission is at the heart of the philosophy of inclusiveness. Society as an ideal of concern for one's fellow man appeals to the same moral insight that condemns society as an instrument of self-interest. There is no reason why social forms cannot be worked for good ends as well as evil ones, and this in fact is the case in the last quarter of *The Golden Bowl*.

This does not mean that the social ideal and the intuitive moral ideal are represented as coinciding, but it does indicate the slightness of James's preference for the latter. The sensitive hero as we have seen him does not satisy all the ideals James admired, after all. Milly Theale, as the purest version of the type, would be utterly unprepared to cope with the real problems that arise in *The Princess Casamassima*. Romantic fantasy is her only mode of thought. The hero, abysmally concerned with his own freedom as he may be, cannot renounce the world without incurring the accusation of neglect of social duty—an accusation which, incidentally, was leveled against James throughout his career. This is a problem that must have been perfectly real to him, especially at a time when his reputation as an ivory-tower dweller was at a disturbing peak. *The Golden Bowl* is perhaps an attempt at juxtaposing— not identifying—the two parts of James's moral awareness, his intuitive inclusiveness and his social conscience. Neither of them can be expected to disgrace the other in the novel's final meaning.

Some such explanation, at any rate, is necessary to an understanding of this novel. The only alternative would be to conclude that James did try to "say things" through its action but that he lost interest, or failed through an overcomplication of poetic effects. This view finds James guilty of sacrificing his moral incisiveness to his love of vagueness and ornamentation. Certainly *The Golden Bowl* exhibits the height of his interest in mystery, innuendo, and elaborate dramatic dialogue, and its characters seem to speak for themselves rather than for their social histories. They are all perceptive and generous, and they appear to act in accordance with their roles in the immediate situation rather than with national or class-ingrained traits. However, these traits have been named and minutely described, and when the action is finished we realize that no other circumstances can explain the radical differences in behavior that the various characters have shown. It is true that by taking all these social factors into account we must see the moral issue as complicated almost to the point of self-contradiction, but perhaps this, again, is an accurate account of "real life" in its broadest aspect. It is certain at any rate that each of the characters in *The Golden Bowl* is allowed to think of his social background so ambiguously that in any given crisis he is "free" of it—i.e. he may choose to obey any one of his numerous, conflicting impulses.

This subtlety of method need not be set down to preciousness on James's part. It can be seen as the culmination of a process we have been tracing all along, the purification of "situation" as a vehicle of meaning. Characters who are not dominated by personal or social idiosyncracies of feeling, but who are able instead to confront their problems with a large measure of detachment, will necessarily tell us more about the real nature of those problems than more predictable characters could. In *The Ambassadors* we found that the absence of absolute, unqualified villains made the social issues clearer rather than less so; Strether was finally able to see the merits and drawbacks of the opposing values without committing himself entirely to one set of characters or another. This was even more apparent in *The Wings of the Dove,* where Densher, far from being physically allied with Milly, whose values he approved, was actually committed to the girl who stood for everything he came to abhor. The fact that he could break this commitment was our measure of the force of his rejection. It was not Milly herself but Milly's principles in the abstract that he affirmed, and he was able to do so pre-cisely because he was superior to any single aspect of his past. This kind of situation has been further intensified in *The Golden Bowl*. Each of the principal characters admires the other three sufficiently for us to be sure that any clash of personality will be determined only by the problem at hand, and everyone regards his social background—the usual basis for motivation in James—with a significant critical reserve. We can no longer predict the behavior of any character. Instead of beginning with the fact of socially determined motivation, as in *The Ambassadors,* and then observing actions which are explainable in those terms, we begin only with the actions, committed by ostensibly free characters, and in retrospect we see their true motivation. If James's immediate reason for this refinement was a desire to escape once and for all from the use of stereotypes, on our own part it should justify a closer attention than ever to the problem of social causality.

2.

Superficially the plot of *The Golden Bowl* is a simple one. Adam Verver, an American multimillionaire with a passion for collecting rare objects, has collected a penniless but authentic Italian prince for his daughter Maggie. Despite the Prince's acquiescence in Maggie's desire to share their existence with Adam, Maggie feels that her marriage has created a disproportion in her otherwise ideal relationship with her father. Adam, while perfectly content for his own sake with things as they stand, perceives Maggie's uneasiness in this respect, and therefore marries a poor but sophisticated American friend of Maggie's, Charlotte Stant, in order to restore the balance. But it turns out that Charlotte and the Prince were lovers before their separate marriages, and that they had failed to marry only because of their mutual poverty. Adam and Maggie, unaware of this, are happy to see their spouses taking such a friendly interest in each other; this leaves them free to indulge in their old father-daughter affection with clear consciences. Charlotte and the Prince thus find themselves tacitly encouraged to renew their illicit relationship. Maggie gradually discovers the true state of affairs, and takes matters into her own hands. The remainder of the book is occupied with each character's attempt to find out how much the others know and with Maggie's efforts to avoid a disastrous rupture. Only Adam seems untroubled, and the other three find themselves dedicated, for various reasons, to saving him from knowledge. The book ends with the Verver couple sailing off to live in America, thus removing the cause of trouble. Maggie and the Prince are now presumably ready to live happily ever after. However, a great number of questions have been left hanging in various stages of resolution.

The subject of the novel, in my opinion, is power. What is its nature? Who possesses it? What are its moral implications? These, I think, are the questions posed with the deepest urgency. Each of the characters is seeking control over the others, or resisting their control, or deliberately acquiescing in it. Each has the matter of social dominance in the front of his consciousness. The four main characters represent four distinct kinds of power, and the motion of the book is a gradual shift in emphasis from the power of one character to that of another. We come to recognize the power of each, but realize with every change of focus that the person now under observation is stronger than his predecessor. At the end of the novel we have made out fairly well who is the most powerful character and why. The final and greatest exercise of power dissolves the situation which called for a test in the first place.

The person who seems at once to be most powerful is Adam Verver, for he has amassed the greatest wealth. However, we are prevented from contemplating the size and nature of his influence, in the early books, by James's refusal to bring him into the foreground; the first object of our attention is Prince Amerigo, Maggie's husband. The Prince enjoys power of a peculiar and seemingly limited nature. He enters the story with only his pedigree as a social asset; the hard cash which should ideally accompany it is lacking. Furthermore, his noble birth stands for certain dangerous restrictions in his adaptability. As he remarks to Maggie, "I'm like a chicken, at best, chopped up and smothered in sauce; cooked down as a *crème de volaille,* with half the parts left out. Your father's the natural fowl running about the *bassecour.*"[1] His consciousness of his value as an object of curiosity interferes with his ability to deal with people on any other basis. He cannot maneuver freely.

However, the Prince's attraction as a museum piece ought not to be underestimated, for it gains him an access to the very type of power he has lacked. If he enters the story only with an inherited charm, he quickly turns it into a large monetary capital. Adam Verver, wealthy as he is, feels incomplete without the polish and leisure that Amerigo represents, and his "collection" of Amerigo gives the Prince a unique freedom:

It was as if he had been some old embossed coin, of a purity of gold no longer used, stamped with glorious arms, mediaeval, wonderful, of which the "worth" in mere modern change, sovereigns and half-crowns, would be great enough, but as to which, since there were finer ways of using it, such taking to pieces was superfluous. That was the image for the security in which it was open to him to rest; he was to constitute a possession, yet was to escape being reduced to his component parts. What would this mean but that, practically, he was never to be tried or tested? [*1,* 23f.]

Thus his real power consists in his invulnerability to the destructive influence of others. In addition, he has the valuable art of making himself liked by men and, even better, loved by women. His power in this regard over Fanny Assingham, the *ficelle,* was his passport to the

---

1. Henry James, *The Golden Bowl* (2 vols. in one, New York, Grove Press, 1952), *1,* 8.

Ververs' acquaintance in the first place, and his immediate influence over Maggie made Fanny's matchmaking possible. At several points in the novel he uses Maggie's attraction to him as a means of controlling her thoughts, just as he does, less conspicuously, with Charlotte. Nor does he fail to employ his aristocratic composure as a means of defense when the main crisis of the novel occurs. His very graciousness and apparent lack of ambition, coupled with his access to Adam's wealth and Maggie's "extraordinary American good faith" (1, 11), make him a hard man to overpower.

Charlotte Stant also comes to life early in the novel, but we are not impressed with her power until the third of the six books into which *The Golden Bowl* is divided. This is because she remains financially poor, and hence an object of pity, until that time. But our interest in power gradually leads us from Amerigo to her, for she proves herself clearly superior to him. She too acquires some of Adam's wealth by being "collected," although her appeal is more fortuitous than the Prince's. She luckily answers the description of a wife for Adam who will be able to get along with all three parties and avoid the vulgar appearance of fortune hunting. Once she is accepted in this role she displays a versatility and courage that Amerigo cannot match. Whereas Amerigo's power is all for resistance, Charlotte is capable of swift and positive action.

Even before her windfall Charlotte gives indications of an admirable strength of will. Despite her poverty she has always managed to preserve her dignity and to command respect. She has, as Maggie notes, something about her "that carries things off." (1, 187) She is naturally adapted to a world where acquisition of money is a primary goal. James's imagery never illustrates this more effectively than in Amerigo's opinion of Charlotte's figure, suggesting the union of sexual and fiscal power: "He knew above all the extraordinary fineness of her flexible waist . . . which gave her a likeness also to some long, loose silk purse, well filled with gold pieces, but having been passed, empty, through a finger-ring that held it together." (1, 49) When her cunning does not remind one of a snake, her boldness suggests larger beasts. Like Kate and Maud she is repeatedly compared to some lithe, single-minded, predatory animal. Her power is further enhanced by an ability to bring a gentler aspect into view. "If when she moved off she looked like a huntress, she looked when she came nearer like . . . a muse." (1, 49) Intelligence, ruthlessness, and social poise are her capital. As soon as she takes the initiative in renewing her old relationship with the comparatively timid Amerigo, we are convinced of her superior power. Throughout Part III and in most of Part IV we see Charlotte outmaneuvering the other characters with the greatest facility.

Before Part IV is quite over, however, we are subjected to another and more sudden shift in focus. Maggie has stumbled upon Charlotte's and Amerigo's secret, and with the aid of the repentant Fanny Assingham she brings herself to face the conclusion that things have turned out badly. Now Maggie steps into the spotlight, and remains there permanently. Her power, which is radically different from that of either Charlotte or Amerigo, gradually makes itself felt as greater than either of theirs. Like Amerigo's it is a capacity chiefly for preserving rather than acquiring, yet it has no basis in any venerable tradition. "The only geography marking it [her 'place'] would be doubtless that of the fundamental passions." (1, 332) Like Milly Theale's, her strength is her ability to love and forgive. But it differs from Milly's in two essential respects. First, it is a power for self-redemption as well as for the redemption of others. Milly, as a visitor from another spiritual world, had neither the ability nor the need for personal salvation. She merely suffered and died, without having participated in worldly sins. But Maggie is involved in a dilemma for which she herself is partially responsible, and however much she may be working to save the others, she is primarily saving herself. Secondly, and similarly, Maggie's power is much more tangible than Milly's. Although she too appears as a figure of generous innocence—hence gaining Amerigo's firm loyalty in the two final sections of the book—she also exercises direct social power on Charlotte's level. Her discretion and patience are apparently limitless, and she has a sure feeling for the proper moment to make herself felt. She can be ruthless when necessary. Furthermore, her general aspect of innocence and good will is an element of power. Because she appears to be naïve on a colossal scale and is willing to maintain this appearance even after she has discovered the truth, she can prevent her opponents from dealing with her on the basis of accepted knowledge. In fact, the other characters are unanimous in feeling that it would be criminal to disenchant so innocent a girl. Even after she has taken Amerigo into her confidence Maggie is able to keep Charlotte in confusion about the degree of her understanding of the affair. In addition to the power of Adam's wealth, which stands squarely if unobtrusively behind every step that she takes, she has the double weapon of social presence and spiritual inaccessibility. Charlotte turns out to be no match for her.

Power, then, is seen to consist in several virtues, both Christian and Machiavellian, but above all in the virtue of not letting one's antagonists know what is on one's mind. Maggie is superior to both Charlotte and Amerigo in this respect. But if inscrutability is the key to power, no one can deny that Adam Verver holds that key. This is the truth that becomes increasingly plain as the novel unfolds, until at the finish everyone has discovered for himself that Adam is supreme. He not only is the chief source of their own power, but has a great amount of it reserved to himself—more than anyone is capable of guessing. His success depends on just this ability to mask his strength. As he reflects, "Everyone has need of one's power, whereas one's own need, at the best, would have seemed to be but some trick for not communicating it." (1, 132) Adam succeeds, where even Maggie fails, in remaining altogether out of the foreground. He paces quietly across "the further end of any watched perspective" (2, 339), making no demands, asking no questions, but merely reminding the others of his presence. His raw power—that is to say, the other characters' estimation of his power— is sufficiently eloquent in itself.

Adam's success is in three fields: the art of making money, the hobby of collecting precious things, and family harmony. His method is identical in all three areas. He neutralizes his own feelings and concerns himself only with satisfying the feelings of others.

... this amiable man bethought himself of his personal advantage, in general, only when it might appear to him that other advantages, those of other persons, had successfully put in their claim. It may be mentioned also that he always figured other persons ... as a numerous array, and that, though conscious of but a single near tie, one affection, one duty deepest-rooted in his life, it had never, for many minutes together, been his portion not to feel himself surrounded and committed, never quite been his refreshment to make out where the many-coloured human appeal ... really faded to the blessed impersonal whiteness for which his vision sometimes ached. [1, 127]

James presents this as the functioning of Adam's generous nature, and suggests (very uncharacteristically) that we look upon Adam's case with an attention "tender indeed almost to compassion." (1, 127) In one sense this is meant seriously; Adam does take elaborate pains for other people's comfort, and is always anxious to do the right thing. But this subjection to conscience has not prevented him from interpreting "other advantages" as strangely identical with his own. Although he regards himself whimsically as a martyr, it would be no further from the truth to say that he has actually been a plunderer. James brings this out by likening him to Cortez, and even his attraction to rare objects is seen in this light: "To rifle the Golden Isles had, on the spot, become the business of his future . . ." (1, 142) Adam makes no distinction between collecting objects and collecting people. He observes his grand prize, Amerigo, with a regard "much of the same order as any glance directed, for due attention . . . to the figure of a cheque received in the course of business and about to be enclosed to a banker." (1, 330) His financial sense is the deepest current in his life, and it governs his behavior on all levels: "he was, as a taster of life, economically constructed." (1, 199) However, this bias has not kept him from indulging his aesthetic sense. He has simply taken care not to let his taste interfere with his business acumen. "Adam Verver had in other words learnt the lesson of the senses, to the end of his own little book, without having, for a day, raised the smallest scandal in his economy at large; being in this particular not unlike those fortunate bachelors, or other gentlemen of pleasure, who so manage their entertainment of compromising company that even the austerest housekeeper, occupied and competent below-stairs, never feels obliged to give warning." (1, 200f.) His very leisure to collect works of art is made possible by his highly efficient financial sense, a sharpness so instinctive that it leaves his conscious mind free for other pleasures—pleasures which, admittedly, are scarcely different to him from the pleasure of making money.

One of the central facts about power in *The Golden Bowl* is that a pose of utter unconcern for one's self is the surest means of getting what one wants. Actual unconcern, which Adam is far from possessing, is not so efficacious. Adam has disciplined himself to behave as if nothing mattered to him, with the consequence that one can neither "talk him up" when selling to him nor question the fairness of his price when buying. For himself, emotion is systematically banished from his mind. His every effort is toward cultivating the appearance of perfect ambiguity. His eyes, for example, present the uncertainty "of your scarce knowing if they most carried their possessor's vision out or most opened themselves to your own." (1, 173) Or again, this austere reflection: "Variety of imagination—what is that but fatal, in the world of affairs, unless so disciplined as not to be distinguished from monotony?" (*1*, 129) Adam has made himself deliberately monotonous in dress and manner. His attitude—and the Prince is correct in insisting, at an early point, that Adam does possess one—is reflected in "his so marked peculiarity of seeming on no occasion to *have* an attitude." (*2*, 366)

Only in his relationship with Maggie does he indulge his affections at all. Maggie is the principal joy of his life, and he shows a true generosity to her. Self-interest in this case is exactly equivalent to making Maggie comfortable. Even this indulgence, of course, is backed by his perception that Maggie is completely loyal to him, and Maggie actually helps him in his effort to conceal his power from others. She treats him like a helpless old man, or rather like a helpless, innocent child: "She kissed him, she arranged his cravat, she dropped remarks, she guided him out, she held his arm, not to be led, but to lead him, and taking it to her by much the same intimate pressure she had always used, when a little girl, to mark the inseparability of her doll . . ."[2] (*2*, 86) This childhood image is one of many that are associated with the Ververs, and especially with Adam. He and Maggie are often likened to an infant king and queen—that is, to rulers of harmless and cherubic countenance but of limitless untouched power. The whole social game they are playing occasionally receives similar treatment, as, for example, when Charlotte and Maggie are likened to "children playing at paying visits" (*1*, 254) or when Maggie reveals her complex insights to Fanny "very much as a wise, or even a mischievous, child, playing on the floor, might pile up blocks, skilfully and dizzily, with an eye on the face of a covertly-watching elder." (*2*, 106) Such imagery suggests more than that the situation of the novel is in essence a game one wins or loses by making moves. It brings out the feeling that the characters themselves, as individuals, are not really identical with or responsible for their observed power. The Ververs in particular handle themselves with oblivious ease, like children who do not really know or care what they are doing. The child does not ask where his blocks came from, he just sits down and plays with them. The same is true of the infant ruler: he has at his fingertips a magical influence for which he has neither worked, nor worried, nor suffered. Adam has access to

---

2. This passage has a significant context. Maggie is on the verge of sacrificing continued life with Adam to the preservation of her marriage, and Adam, fully conscious of her problem and sympathetic with her decision, is allowing himself to be sacrificed. His positive decision is concealed in his deliberate appearance of passivity.

power like the energy of the machines that made him wealthy; he simply presses the right button, and his streamlined American personality does the rest. A child could operate him.[3]

3.

Remembering our qualification that all the characters in *The Golden Bowl* behave as if they were free, we must now look for hints of their true motivation. The character who is most obviously a product of her class is Fanny Assingham—not the most subtle of James's symbolic names. She is an American who has married a stodgy and unimaginative army colonel, a sort of English Waymarsh; James compares him to Attila the Hun. Fanny has an active mind and heart and a taste for matchmaking. However, social respectability is the one touchstone of her life, the goal she seems always, through overdressing and oversympathizing with her superiors, just barely to be reaching. She moves among the Ververs with precariousness, for everyone is aware that she is not their social equal. Indeed, for one period in the novel she is mercilessly excluded from their company, and she is only reinstated when her usefulness has been re-established. Although she is by no means an entirely sympathetic figure, her comic ambivalence between American simplicity and an equally American desire to be sophisticated makes for an occasionally touching picture. "With her false indolence . . . her false leisure, her false pearls and palms and courts and fountains, she was a person for whom life was multitudinous detail, detail that left her, as it at any moment found her, unappalled and unwearied." Childless and penniless, she compensates for her wants by "dropping social scraps into them." (*1, 36*) Her deeds in the novel suggest an ambiguity of motive between her affection for the other characters and her desire to borrow their social luster—and as usual, James does not resolve the ambiguity.

Fanny is the only character whose social background is discussed with brutal frankness by the others, without the sense that such im-

3. In *The American Scene* (1907) James likens the social atmosphere of New York to that of a debutante party: "The confidence and innocence are those of children whose world has ever been practically a safe one, and the party so imaged is thus really even a child's party . . ." He then goes on to generalize: "it comes home to the restless analyst everywhere that this 'childish' explanation is the one that meets the greatest number of the social appearances. . . . The immensity of the native accommodation, socially speaking, for the childish life, is not that exactly the key of much of the spectacle?" (New York, Scribner's, 1946), pp. 170f.

personal facts really don't matter. But her friends are "explained" too, the only difference being that they are spared James's directly satirical approach. Prince Amerigo is perhaps the most "fixed" of all. He belongs to a type "about which everything is known." (*1*, 12) Yet even here James will not be pinned down, for Amerigo is not altogether content with his background. He disavows the historical scandals of his Italian forebears, and his marriage to Maggie is seen partly as a gesture of escape from the past. "What was this so important step he had just taken but the desire for some new history that should, so far as possible, contradict, and even if need be flatly dishonour, the old?" (*1*, 17) Amerigo is conscious of the freedom and innocence, as well as the financial solvency, of the New World—a composite virtue he chooses to call "science." To be scientific is to belong to the future, and to live in the future is Amerigo's ideal. He has decided that the only way to surmount a tradition of immorality which has revolved around money and power is to become effortlessly rich and powerful himself.

Thus Amerigo too has an ambivalence of motive. His reasons for wanting Adam Verver's money are both selfish and idealistic. His idealism is not incongruous with his heritage but is rather a reaction against it, a desire for expiation. He tries to adjust himself completely to Adam's modern industrial, "scientific" world, but his background will not be dismissed: "Its presence in him was like the consciousness of some inexpugnable scent in which his clothes, his whole person, his hands and the hair of his head, might have been steeped as in some chemical bath: the effect was nowhere in particular, yet he constantly felt himself at the mercy of the cause." (*1*, 16) Although he has used this quality to great profit in his courtship of Maggie, it limits his sense of reality. "He liked all signs that things were well, but he cared rather less *why* they were." (*1*, 140) This is the result of an ancestral freedom from practical worries, but the freedom has ebbed away and left him stranded. Amerigo's marriage into the New World is an effort to restore the power that made his freedom possible in the first place.

Charlotte Stant's situation is much the same as the Prince's; she clings to the Ververs to "stay afloat" socially. However, there is a significant difference in her background. Whereas Amerigo's heritage has left him helpless but socially valuable, Charlotte's has made her versatile but unimposing. In Maggie's words, she "hasn't a creature in the world really—that is nearly—belonging to her. Only acquaintances who, in all sorts of ways, make use of her, and distant relations who are so afraid she'll make use of *them* that they seldom let her look at them." (*1,* 184) Her pitiful Italian-American past, somewhat like Milly Theale's wasted life, does provide her with a modest appeal: "Her singleness, her solitude, her want of means, that is her want of ramifications and other advantages, contributed to enrich her somehow with an odd, precious neutrality, to constitute for her, so detached yet so aware, a sort of small social capital." (*1,* 56) But her shabby Tuscan childhood and her "demoralized, falsified, polyglot" (*1,* 57) American parentage were chiefly important in their sharpening of her adaptability to a world of no permanent values, either social or moral. Charlotte makes up her own rules of behavior, but the very broadness of her choice is dictated by her lack of previous discipline.

The enigmatic and seemingly omnipotent Adam Verver is no less restricted by his social background than Charlotte is. His power, as we saw, derives from the particular commercial society of his homeland. Even taking this power at face value we must recognize that his manipulation of it is characteristically American. As Maggie tells Amerigo in the first chapter, Adam is hopelessly and absolutely romantic. James emphasizes at several points that Adam, like Milly, is searching for "the real thing," and furthermore that he is prevented from finding it by his idealism as much as by his being "economically constructed." Not only are his collections, his relationship with Maggie, and his projects for the utopian American City all part of a national obsession with the ideal, they all fall characteristically short of the real. His "lightning elevator" moral sense streaks right past actuality and drops him off at the top floor—from which, for all his good intentions, he can't possibly see the levels below. James is thus at his most ironical when speaking of Adam's perceptiveness. Adam thinks he is combining American simplicity with the taste of a connoisseur of art: "He was a plain American citizen . . . but no Pope, no prince of them all had read a richer meaning, he believed, into the character of the Patron of Art. . . . His freedom to see—of which the comparisons were part— what could it do but steadily grow and grow?" (*1,* 152f.) What he is really doing is admiring an image of himself that he has drawn from his concept of perfection—i.e. from the marriage of power and taste. But if his power is real, we are led to believe that his taste is specious. "He cared that a work of art of price should 'look like' the master to whom it might perhaps be deceitfully attributed; but he had ceased on the whole to know any matter of the rest of life by its looks." (1, 149)

Lack of genuine contact with reality, then, is Adam's principal shortcoming. He is an expert on the relative usefulness of things, but he is incapable of discovering what things *are*. This condition, like his power, derives from his supremely American pragmatism. Indeed, his power and his weakness are two sides of the same coin, for a monotonous vagueness of mind is at the base of them both. His life has simply been a series of Yankee shortcuts to success, and the real Adam Verver, if such a man ever existed, has been dispensed with on the grounds of inefficiency.

The most difficult character to speak of in social terms is not Adam but Maggie—the reason perhaps being that she suggests some of the forbiddingly impressive stature of Milly Theale. Maggie appears for a while to be nothing less than a reincarnation of Milly, and if she later reminds us somewhat of Kate Croy as well, the question of her motivation is only rendered more complicated than before. The most important fact about Maggie is that she is Adam's daughter. She shares his romantic American insistence on idealizing everything she sees, yet at the same time she is intensely concerned to arrive at "the real thing." Amerigo summarizes the uncomfortable paradox by saying that when she does not see too little she sees too much. She manages to substitute a set of romantic symbols for the reality she is looking for. Not the least of these symbols is her own husband, to whom she was immediately attracted on the sentimental grounds that his name suggested Amerigo Vespucci, the link between the Old World and the New. While this has obvious significance for a reading of *The Golden Bowl* as a parable of modern history, it must be taken literally as a reflection on Maggie's tendency to think in terms of myths rather than facts.

As in the case of our previous heroes, Maggie's American emptiness seems to be the source of her moral energy. However, it is also the cause of a serious blind spot. Like Milly, she enters her novel with no interest in the moral rightness or wrongness of attitudes more sophisticated than her own. Amerigo epitomizes Evil Old Europe for her; he is the favorite toy in her collection. She therefore positively expects and looks forward to a corruption in him—she regards corruption as the mark of authenticity. In giving herself over to her childish imagination, the girl who "wasn't born to know evil" (1, 80) unconsciously encourages it. The very strength she finally uses to rescue the other characters is based in part on an inability to comprehend the full scope of the insult that has been offered her. However, this should not be overstressed, for Maggie does succeed, where previous heroes failed, in making an adequate compromise between her ideals and her treatment of the real situation at hand.

This success itself may be traced to social causes. Unlike Milly, Maggie begins not only with money but with property, family, and even "happiness" from the very first. She is more involved because she has more to lose. But again, as in Adam's case, this immeasurable wealth prevents her from being able to define herself adequately. She knows that she must "end" somewhere, but never having once been disappointed in her wishes, she cannot really picture any limit to her influence. Adam's munificence has sheltered her not only from a world of petty worries, but from any true knowledge of herself. The disaster of the novel may be attributed to this fact as neatly as to any other. Not possessing the remotest suspicion that reality cannot be made over to meet her sense of the ideal, she assumes that the quadrangular marriage has solved every difficulty in her life. Amerigo, whose reaction to this attitude is "a strange final irritation" at its naïveté, sees it in a severe light which we must recognize as valid: "He compared the lucid result [his irritation] with the extraordinary substitute for perception that presided, in the bosom of his wife, at so contented a view of his conduct and course—a state of mind that was positively like a vicarious good conscience, cultivated ingeniously on his behalf, a perversity of pressure innocently persisted in." (*1, 339*) Maggie is anything but stupid, yet for half of the novel her intelligence is hopelessly misdirected. In her blindness as well as her strength, Maggie is an accurate representative of her class, her family, and her country.

4.

All the foregoing remarks are a preface to the question we must now ask ourselves: where does moral responsibility lie? Each character in the drama, as we have seen, can point to circumstances in extenuation of his faults, and, conversely, none can point to his virtues without reminding us of happy causes in his background. From the deterministic point of view *The Golden Bowl* ends in moral neutrality. Yet we have also seen that each character manages to transcend or contradict any single trait of country or class that we might choose to emphasize. The Americans are not satisfied—but for typically American reasons—with being merely American, and the same holds true for the Italian Prince.

Although none of the action is "out of character," James has made character itself ambiguous, so that at any given point we cannot say for sure that the motive for an act is selfish or altruistic. Everyone can look back and say with honesty that he has done something constructive about his social limitations.

It is therefore a significant fact that each character admits to a basic sense of guilt. Fanny Assingham is uneasy from the first about having promoted Maggie's marriage to a man whom she knew to be in love with another woman, and in concealing her knowledge of Charlotte's all too adequate credentials for getting along with her prospective son-in-law. She fears that in both cases her motive will be seen as partiality to Amerigo, with whom she is infatuated. Charlotte too is upset about allowing her childhood friend to marry a man whom she knows to be still completely in love with herself. The particular importance she places on the expiatory wedding gift stresses this fact. Amerigo also feels guilty, not about marrying for money but rather for leaving his penniless mistress out of the picture. Maggie feels guilty about having upset her old relationship with Adam, and Adam in return is sorry that he has allowed Maggie to fret over this essentially trivial but disturbing impression.

All this penitence at the outset, in a situation which seems to fall barely short of being ideal for everyone, must strike the reader as evidence of a great and perhaps even excessive moral delicacy. Each character feels it his duty to atone for some oversight, mistake, or coincidence for which he is careful to accept the blame. However, is it true that this constitutes genuine moral insight? Fanny's sin lies not in allowing her motives to be suspected, but in meddling in the first place. She tries to redeem herself only through further meddling. Charlotte has only to tell Maggie of her previous relationship with Amerigo for the marriage to begin on a properly candid basis, but she neglects to do so. Amerigo's conscience does not prevent him from capitalizing on every possible opportunity to deceive the Ververs. And if Maggie and Adam should do penance, surely it is not for any harm they have inflicted on each other. Each character is concerned with preserving the innocence—that is to say the ignorance—of some other character, but none is really interested in his own guilt. The issues are not being faced.

Doesn't this constitute a preliminary judgment on the social microcosm we are asked to enter? Fanny, Charlotte, the Prince, Adam, and Maggie are all guilty of various failings, but each is enabled to sidestep his true responsibility. "Society" itself—the contrived double marriage —is the field in which each is encouraged to ease his conscience falsely. Instead of exposing moral errors, society assimilates them and thrives on them. Everything is converted, hypocritically, into "service for others," while the real truth is hushed and sanctified in accepted social forms. Society as the five characters conceive it is basically a means of circumventing reality. This is especially traceable to the Ververs, for it is they who prescribe the extreme delusions of innocence that Charlotte and Amerigo find themselves expected to preserve. Amerigo, who for all his ambition is the character least at home in an atmosphere of mystery, compares the Ververs' moral climate to a milky fog, a white curtain, and later to a golden mist. At first he sees only the promise of goodness behind this barrier, but he gradually realizes that for the Ververs it is a substitute for regarding the world as it is—a screen for the safe development of "a vicarious good conscience."

However, if we try to fix the blame for confusion on one character or group, we find the evidence insubstantial. Although Adam is the prime mover in this social universe, the other characters, including Amerigo, accept its forms more or less cheerfully as they find them privately advantageous. When Maggie finally comes to perceive the evil that her social world has tolerated, she fixes all the blame on Charlotte and Amerigo rather than on Adam or herself. Whether right or wrong, her judgment captures the deep danger of "good manners" in *The Golden Bowl*: "She saw at all events why horror itself had almost failed her . . . the horror of finding evil seated, all at its ease, where she had only dreamed of good; the horror of the thing hideously *behind*, behind so much trusted, so much pretended, nobleness, cleverness, tenderness. . . . it had met her like some bad-faced stanger surprised in one of the thick-carpeted corridors of a house of quiet on a Sunday afternoon." (2, 243) Society is the bond of genteel, domestic, but quite immoral hypocrisy between all the characters of the novel. Hence we should be able to arrive at a preliminary moral judgment, an assignment of relative moral responsibility, by finding which of the characters contributes the most to this atmosphere of deception.

The answer to this question is certainly not Fanny, Amerigo, or Maggie. Fannie is little more than a naïve messenger between the other characters. She enters the central action only by their invitation, and exerts influence only when they are particularly disposed to receive it. This is not to say that she does not manipulate social forms for her private advantage, but simply that her opportunities for doing so are limited. In her own small way she does her part in maintaining the general cowardice. She finds it inconvenient to believe in the adulterous relationship between Amerigo and Charlotte in the first half of the book, and when she finally makes an effort to atone for this self-deception, it is only because further dissembling has become impracticable. It might also be noted that Fanny was the one who brought Amerigo and the Ververs together in the first place. But if she thus touches off an unpleasant series of developments, we cannot say that she has planned or even anticipated them.

On similar grounds Amerigo himself seems innocent of deep social evil. It is true enough that his Italian conscience, as he admits cheerfully, "is slow and steep and unlighted, with so many of the steps missing that . . . it's as short, in almost any case, to turn round and come down again." (1, 32) Yet this very clarity of analysis is evidence of a moral sense, a self-awareness unknown to the Ververs. Amerigo is a person who seems to depend entirely on the moral initiative of others. He relies first on Fanny, then Maggie, then Adam, then Charlotte, and finally on Maggie again; at no point in the novel does he appear to be standing on his own feet. Of course this should not be confused with passive helplessness—his successes are too carefully timed—but it does suggest that we should look elsewhere for the source of positive evil in *The Golden Bowl*.

As for Maggie, she emerges as the heroine rather than the villain of the book. However, as we have seen, she has limitations of vision that amount almost to a positive willfulness of ignorance. Yet none of her shortcomings may be said to be anything but the result of Adam Verver's influence; insofar as we must condemn her point of view at all, the guilt reverts to Adam. The same is true of Amerigo in his early relationship with Charlotte. In the central drama of the book there are really two moral camps, not four; Adam and Charlotte are the leaders of two opposing attitudes which are merely defended, not formulated or understood, by Maggie and Amerigo respectively. It is to Adam and Charlotte that we must turn for the true sources of action.

This brings us to the most difficult aspect of a moral reading of *The Golden Bowl*, namely the fact that the two major philosophies never come to a direct comparison of worth. Adam's guilt lies entirely in his original creation of a hypocritical, self-satisfied world, whereas Charlotte's lies entirely in her exploitation of that world. Adam's guilt is thus completed, or nearly so, at the beginning of the novel, while Charlotte's develops during the observed action. Unless we are un-usually careful we may be likely to evaluate Charlotte and Adam according to only one of two valid perspectives. If we concentrate chiefly on the action at hand Charlotte will appear guiltier, but if we ask only why such action was made necessary in the first place, we shall blame Adam. There is sufficient evidence that James expected us to see the problem from both points of view, but unfortunately there is no accurate means of subtracting one set of results from the other. The reader is left to decide for himself whether Charlotte or Adam is more to blame.

Charlotte's guilt is difficult to explain away under any deterministic theory, for although she is the character who is most aware of the moral oddity of the quadrangular marriage, she is also the most eager to exploit it. Her professed philosophy is a sort of enlightened fatalism. In her view Maggie has unthinkingly obliged her to become Amerigo's mistress again, and she positively exults in the mistake. The sinister flavor of her triumph derives exactly from her insistence that she has had no other choice. ". . . I'm, by no merit of my own, just fixed—fixed as fast as a pin stuck, up to its head, in a cushion." (*1, 258*) At several points in the novel she hints at a conception of freedom that is close to Madame Merle's. For Charlotte everyone is a victim of his circumstances, and freedom consists only in putting one's self in the way of the most advantageous conditions. James emphasizes the para-dox in this notion by describing it in terms of enslavement and en-snarement. For example, Charlotte and the Prince have been "placed face to face in a freedom that partook, extraordinarily, of ideal per-fection, since the magic web had spun itself without their toil, almost without their touch." (*1, 302*) To be free in a web—what idea could so little suggest the kind of freedom to which James's best heroes as-pire? Charlotte's supposed fatalism is contradicted at every point by her shrewd, deceitful, and altogether opportunistic manipulation of the Ververs' society. Like Kate Croy she makes her own luck, and she no less than Kate must be held responsible for the low ethics that she uses.

Nevertheless, Adam strikes me as sharing this responsibility. As he admits to himself, he has deliberately used Charlotte as a means of improving his relationship with Maggie: "They [he and Maggie] had brought her in . . . to do the 'worldly' for them, and she had done it with such genius that they had themselves in consequence renounced

it even more than they had originally intended." (*1*, 324) Adam thinks
of this as part of his "moral lucidity" (*1*, 212), but it gives the careful
reader an exactly opposite impression. It presupposes that one can be
vicariously inclusive by hiring other people to do one's living. Furthermore, it is evidence of a serious inconsistency in Adam's view of the
other characters. Although he feels morally obliged to render Maggie's
life as happy and innocent as possible, this very obligation as he conceives it makes him see his other friends only in terms of their usefulness to his plan. This error of vision—the development of the
novel demonstrates that it *is* an error—brought Charlotte to his attention in the first place, and is at least partly the cause of her deceiving
him. He *wants* to be deceived. He implicitly strikes the bargain of ex-
changing a share of his wealth for the privilege of not being told that
his pampering of Maggie is unrealistic. When Charlotte at the end of
the book finds herself compelled to go off to American City, where
people are so awfully "interesting" because so awfully uncivilized, she
is in effect being sent into exile from her imagination. For American
City is the most childish of Adam's projects. "It hadn't merely, his
plan, all the sanctions of civilization; it was positively civilization condensed, concrete, consummate, set down by his hands as a house on a
rock—a house from whose open doors and windows, open to grateful,
to thirsty millions, the higher, the highest knowledge would shine out
to bless the land." (*1*, 147) I should emphasize that American City *will*
be of great value, so far as anyone can tell; but surely Adam exaggerates
his ability to "condense" the experience of centuries for mass consump-
tion. He is capable of enormous good, but by the same token he can
inspire the lowest kind of hypocrisy. Although we see his power for
goodness at work in the second half of the novel, I think that some of
the opposite force is responsible for the initial confusion. Adam's
power is amoral in itself, as we shall see; its use depends more on
Maggie than on himself. But certainly we cannot pass over the fact
that if he had not entered the book with a lack of respect for everyone
but Maggie, the whole fantastic game of deception could never have
been started.

5.

So far I have spoken of *The Golden Bowl* as if it contained no overt
action. It is certainly true that very little movement is to be observed.
However, this lends weight to the one scene in which a violent act is

committed. The scene is that in which Maggie asserts her control of the situation, and the violent act is Fanny Assingham's smashing of the symbolic golden bowl. The bowl had been the subject of one early scene, but has been virtually forgotten until this occasion. It was the gift that Charlotte had intended to buy for Maggie as a wedding present. Charlotte and the antique dealer who owned the cup were both anxious for the sale, but Amerigo had objected on the grounds that it was a misleading present: it was made of crystal, not gold, and the crystal had a hidden flaw in it. The following exchange between Charlotte and the shopkeeper illustrates the symbolic value that becomes attached to the bowl:

> "Does one make a present," she asked, "of an object that contains, to one's knowledge, a flaw?"
>
> "Well, if one knows of it one has only to mention it. The good faith," the man smiled, "is always there."
>
> "And leave the person to whom one gives the thing, you mean, to discover it?"
>
> "He wouldn't discover it . . . He might know—and he might try. But he wouldn't find."
>
> She kept her eyes on him as if, though unsatisfied, mystified, she yet yet had a fancy for the bowl. "Not even if the thing should come to pieces?" And then as he was silent: "Not even if he should have to say to me 'The Golden Bowl is broken'?"
>
> He was still silent; after which he had his strangest smile. "Ah, if anyone should *want* to smash it—!" [*1,* 119f.]

The bowl symbolizes the defective marriage between Maggie and the Prince. Everything would be made right if Maggie were informed at the start that there existed a "flaw" in Amerigo's role of the innocent bridegroom. Maggie would never locate this particular weakness in his past, but at least she would be on her guard against "breakage," and the marriage would be operationally sound. Only if someone should place deliberate stress on the flaw would the general harmony be endangered.

Each character has a significant relationship to the bowl. Amerigo reveals his uneasy conscience when he insists that the gift not be presented at all, either to Maggie or (Charlotte's second idea) to himself. Charlotte, in contrast, likes the bowl but can't afford it. The idea of exploiting Amerigo's new situation, however morally defective that situation may be, appeals to her, but until she can marry Adam she is helpless. Adam himself is linked to the bowl in elaborate image patterns of gold and crystal, suggesting that he too has a share in its flaw. His money is the source of the marriage, and his influence behind the scenes is the force that keeps the truth from being expressed. As for Fanny and Maggie, neither of them has heard of the bowl until Maggie buys it in Part IV, and learns from the shopkeeper that Charlotte considered buying it for Amerigo on the eve of his wedding. This confirms her long-nurtured suspicions about the adultery. Fanny, who knew of the "flaw" and hence now sees the bowl as a symbol of her own guilt, breaks it into three pieces by smashing it against the floor.

This act may signal that Fanny wants the truth to be faced and the false situation dissolved, or that she is trying to belittle the whole idea of a treachery. In any case, it is Maggie's reaction that is important. Maggie has perceived all she needs in order to condemn Charlotte and Amerigo, and as Amerigo dramatically enters the room and asks what significance she had placed on the now shattered bowl, Maggie makes her great decision. She picks up the fragments—finding, however, that she can only carry two at a time—and confronts the fact that they *are* fragments:

> She brought them over to the chimney-piece, to the conspicuous place occupied by the cup before Fanny's appropriation of it, and, after laying them carefully down, went back for what remained, the solid detached foot. With this she returned to the mantel-shelf, placing it with deliberation in the centre and then, for a minute, occupying herself as with the attempt to fit the other morsels together. The split, determined by the latent crack, was so sharp and so neat that if there had been anything to hold them the bowl might still, quite beautifully, a few steps away, have passed for uninjured. But, as there was, naturally, nothing to hold them but Maggie's hands, during the few moments the latter were so employed, she could only lay the almost equal parts of the vessel carefully beside their pedestal and leave them thus before her husband's eyes. [2, 189f.]

From now until the end she sees her responsibility clearly. She has shown Amerigo that she knows the whole truth, and her retribution stops right there. Something has made her decide not to humiliate him and the others, but to spare them.

At first we may suspect that this something is her desire to save Adam from a knowledge that would convince him of her unhappiness, but we gradually realize that a stronger motive is at work. This is her heretofore unnoticed love for her husband. Even though she is now disenchanted with him morally, she finds that her love remains unaffected. She later explains to Adam the source of her patience: "My idea is this, that when you only love a little you're naturally not jealous . . . But when you love in a deeper and intenser way, then you are, in the same proportion, jealous . . . When, however, you love in the most abysmal and unutterable way of all—why then you're beyond everything, and nothing can pull you down." (2, 270) This last kind of love has such a hold on Maggie that she eventually sacrifices even the presence of Adam in order to keep Amerigo.

With the extraordinary revelation of his wife's magnanimity Amerigo realizes how unfairly he has been judging her. He has confused the smallness of her social vision with a total moral pettiness, an inability to be selfless. Now he sees that Maggie possesses unsounded depths of understanding and forgiveness that Charlotte can neither match nor appreciate. Contrite, he instantly becomes as thoroughly dedicated to Maggie's point of view as he had recently been to Charlotte's.

Society now begins to look less wicked than when we last evaluated it. In the form of the marital quadrangle it was a protector of false values, and was therefore susceptible to being morally equated with the insufficiency of those values. But now Maggie has isolated the disease from the body. From the moment she has decided that Charlotte and Amerigo must be let off as easily as possible, society becomes an instrument of positive good. The identical function it performed before, that of keeping the bald truth from being expressed, is now a crucial virtue. Maggie realizes that the breakage in the bowl need stand "merely for the dire deformity of her attitude" (2, 246f.) toward the others. By suppressing her wrath and maintaining the social appearance of harmony she can avoid any disastrous confessions or reprisals, and hence salvage the broken pieces of her marriage. If no outward signs of discord are emitted, no one will dare show his hand by acknowledging the existence of that discord. Decorum thus enforces a precious silence, a benevolent hypocrisy.

This new policy of Maggie's is the most important shift in the novel's action, for it establishes the social ideal of harmony as a worthy object for the full American intensity of soul. Harmony of a corrupted sort has been the goal that everyone has promoted until this point; it was a harmony of moral deception. But now each character knows that at least one of the others is aware of his secret. Instead of paying lip service to idealistic standards of impossible purity, the characters are encouraged to work for the saving of their human situation. People, not ideas, become the things worth preserving. In the complex, sensitive world of her personal relationships Maggie has seen that to destroy evil one must also destroy good, since the two are inseparably joined in the human beings at hand. She has come to love people for what they are, good and bad qualities together, rather than for what they should ideally be. She has learned to accommodate evil. In other words, she has learned to *live*.

This transformation puts her in bold relief. Although the motive for her new attitude is the plausible one of preserving what she loves, it also takes on richer meanings. We now see her as beneficent almost in the abstract. Her resolution is "not to give up" the others:

> They thus tacitly put it upon her to be disposed of, the whole complexity of their peril, and she promptly saw why: because she was there, and there just *as* she was, to lift it off them and take it; to charge herself with it as the scapegoat of old . . . [But] it wouldn't be their feeling that she should do anything but live, live on somehow for their benefit, and even as much as possible in their company, to keep proving to them that they had truly escaped and that she was still there to simplify. [2, 240f.]

The last 200 pages of the novel are packed with similar religious suggestions. Maggie at times appears to be acting not so much on her own behalf as in the interest of her sinful companions—and by extension, in the interest of mankind as a whole.

Thus we arrive at a critical problem of great delicacy. It is impossible to speak of an ultimate meaning in *The Golden Bowl* without accounting for the wealth of Christian overtones that James has suggested, and which make themselves heard with increasing stress as the novel draws to a close. To take James's scriptural allusions literally, as evidence that *The Golden Bowl* was written as a religious allegory rather than a novel, would be ill-advised; it would be to contradict all of James's expressed sentiments about the relation of art to truth, to say nothing of his statements about this particular book. On the other hand, it would be equally imprudent to ignore the allusions altogether. Maggie is surrounded with images linking her to Christ, and her own stature as an agent of mercy becomes increasingly great, until at the end she is scarcely human at all. As R. P. Blackmur remarks in his preface, "Maggie Verver is in intention rather like Beatrice in the *Divine Comedy*, the Lady of Theology, and suffers the pangs of the highest human love." (p. x) We saw that Milly Theale was similarly regarded at the end of *The Wings of the Dove*. However, in both cases James has exercised his right to criticize his "divine" heroine implicitly on the basis of purely human failings. We shall see that with Maggie, and equally with Adam, Charlotte, and the Prince, the religious parallels are often contradictory in spirit to James's moral suggestions. Although it is possible to take this as a sign that James no longer cared about morality, it is more probable that he was simply asking us to bring a more than usual attention to bear on his subject. By enlarging his characters through religious analogies he introduced the whole Christian system as an available means of moral judgment. Remembering that nothing is said in *The Golden Bowl* that is not the result of one or another imperfect character's observation, we ought to maintain a willingness to see some of the religious overtones as hypocritical or ironical. In *The Wings of the Dove* Kate Croy all but deified Milly in speech, yet she never arrived at a true appreciation of Milly's love. A similar type of overstatement seems to be operating in *The Golden Bowl*.

The Christlike size of Maggie's love is hinted as early as Part IV, when she is conversing with Fanny:

> ". . . I *am* mild. I can bear anything."
> "Oh, 'bear'!" Mrs. Assingham fluted.
> "For love," said the Princess.
> Fanny hesitated. "Of your father?"
> "For love," Maggie repeated.
> It kept her friend watching. "Of your husband?"
> "For love," Maggie said again. [2, 120]

This same kind of absolutism reappears in her scene with Amerigo and the broken bowl. Instead of taking advantage of her husband's discomposure, she makes the situation as easy as possible for him: "There it was that her wish for time interposed—time for Amerigo's use, not for hers, since she, for ever so long now, for hours and hours as they seemed, had been living with eternity; with which she would continue to live." (2, 191) When the brilliant "card game" scene in Part V offers Maggie a direct challenge to martyr herself, these suggestions become impossible for us to ignore. Maggie wanders in the garden at night and wrestles briefly with her soul, deciding that "giving them up was, marvellously, not to be thought of." (2, 244) When she is about to be confronted by Charlotte with a full demand for redemption, a transference of Charlotte's guilt to her own shoulders, she turns, significantly, to her father.

> Straighter than ever, thus, the Princess again felt it all put upon her, and there was a minute, just a supreme instant, during which there burned in her a wild wish that her father would only look up. It throbbed for these seconds as a yearning appeal to him—she would chance it, that is, if he would but just raise his eyes and catch them [Charlotte and Amerigo], across the larger space, standing in the outer dark together. Then he might be affected by the sight, taking them as they were; he might make some sign—she scarce knew what—that would save *her;* save her from being the one, this way, to pay all. He might . . . out of pity for her, signal to her that this extremity of her effort for him was more than he asked. That represented Maggie's one little lapse from consistency—the sole small deflection in the whole course of her scheme. [2, 251f.]

This "lapse from consistency" may correspond to a trace of human reluctance opposing Christ's resolution to be martyred, or it may refer to His one "inconsistent" cry: "Why hast thou forsaken me?" But in any case the passage is doubly important for the light in which it places Adam Verver. If Maggie reminds us of Christ, surely Adam is here likened to God Himself. This may be a hard position to accept even provisionally, but Maggie's suggestions are too straightforward to be doubted. Maggie has perceived that Adam is the source of her own strength. "The sense that he wasn't a failure, and could never be, purged their predicament of every meanness—made it as if they had really emerged, in their transmuted union, to smile almost without pain. . . . Wasn't it because now, also, on his side, he was thinking of her as his daughter, was *trying* her, during these mute seconds, as the child of his blood? . . . his strength was her strength, her pride was his . . ." (2, 282) This is not to say that Adam is literally divine; it means simply that all of Maggie's love is made possible by her faith in his competence. As she states with emphasis, "I believe in you more than any one." (2, 282) On the level of the drama Maggie's redemptive power has nothing mystical about it, any more than Adam's financial power does. But the world of *The Golden Bowl* is a tiny one, and in a real sense Adam may be called its God and Maggie its Christ. Adam's formlessness, colorlessness, and inaccessibility are, as we saw, the very essence of his power, and this power is seemingly unlimited. Adam "created" the world that Charlotte, Amerigo, and Maggie inhabit; his money is the *primum mobile* of everything that happens in the novel.

But Adam, like the Christian God, cannot turn his power to human love except by representing himself in flesh. This is Maggie's role. As soon as she has decided that her sinful friends deserve "saving" from the situation in which they have placed themselves, Adam's power flows through Maggie and into the others, redeeming and regenerating them. As Fanny recognizes, the real credit for success must revert to Adam. He is, I gather, the "solid detached foot" of the bowl (p. 103, above), without which the other two pieces (Maggie and the Prince) cannot stay together.

Charlotte seems to take at least four roles in this symbolic pattern. In the garden scene she and Amerigo, "standing in the outer dark together," seem to represent a wayward mankind whose sins will be unburdened by Christ. However, the deceitful nature of her appeal and the sinister note in her tone after Maggie has assured her of safety suggest rather that she might be a Judas, and the analogy is virtually confirmed when she ends the scene by kissing Maggie. At several points she also reminds us of the devil, or at least of a woman possessed by devils in the Hawthornian sense. Her voice sounds at one point like "the shriek of a soul in pain" (*2, 300*), and in the garden she behaves with an inhuman foreknowledge of where she should move and what she should say. Finally, her fourth and most heavily emphasized analogy seems to be with a false religious attitude, possibly Judaism. Religious overtones had crept into her "sacred" relationship with Amerigo as early as Part III (e.g. *1, 316*), reminding us that this union was not simply a defiance of Maggie's righteous attitude but an assertion of a positive religious philosophy. This philosophy is simply an eye for an eye, and Charlotte enacts it faithfully throughout the novel. Some of James's occasional imagery reinforces this value in Charlotte —as, for example, when her presence during one of Adam's purchases fitted in so well with "the touch of some mystic rite of old Jewry." (*2, 219*) Although heathen images sometimes replace Jewish ones, the opposition remains distinct between an "unredeemed" view and Maggie's Christian one. Maggie's victory over Charlotte thus constitutes a melting of graven idols. The historical fact of the New Law seems to be implied in *The Golden Bowl's* sequence of dominant attitudes.

However, I should state at once that Charlotte appears more rather than less sympathetic as Maggie's victory becomes more certain. Nor does Adam, the ultimate dispenser of love, seem any less mercenary and narrow-minded than he was at the start. If we follow the religious parallels too closely we end in absurdities. The "fall" of Charlotte and Amerigo was little more than an acceptance of terms implicitly dictated by Adam; he saves them from the consequences of a sin for which he himself is partly responsible. His power remains a matter of hard cash, and his behavior toward the defeated Charlotte is not merciful but cruel. Instead of redeeming her from the world he takes her off to live in a parody of it. American City, Adam's "house on a rock," is not the True Church but rather, one imagines, a Babel of impracticable ideals, a place where money buys not culture and comfort but only more money. Perhaps, then, a fifth role for Charlotte might be that of an Eve, banished into a world of ugliness.

Yet if Charlotte seems damned, Amerigo seems truly saved. His happy reunion with Maggie at the end can be seen as the remarriage of man with divinity, and their son, the Principino, as the first man to be liberated from original sin. The Prince has been cleansed of his evil defect and is now free to live with Christ—in other words, to love Maggie altogether. Significantly, the final step in his salvation depends only on himself; Maggie "had thrown the dice, but his hand was over her cast." (2, 376) As the representative of Europe's oldest culture he successfully adjusts himself to the raw energy of the New World, and becomes subject, equally, to the New Law of love.

But once again we must distinguish between Adam Verver's world and a truly Christian one. The sincerity and strength of Maggie's love cannot be doubted, but its source is in a "God" whose very power derives from a moral oblivion, a completely impersonal attitude; and Maggie, for all the scope of her love, gives her endorsement to this attitude. This is apparent, for example, when Adam and Maggie take symbolic stock of their assets at the end of the book. Charlotte and Amerigo appear to them as mere captives, items in a collection:

The two noble persons seated, in conversation, at tea, fell thus into the splendid effect and the general harmony: Mrs. Verver and the Prince fairly "placed" themselves, however unwittingly, as high expressions of the kind of human furniture required, esthetically, by such a scene. The fusion of their presence with the decorative elements, their contribution to the triumph of selection, was complete and admirable; though, to a lingering view, a view more penetrating than the occasion really demanded, they also might have figured as concrete attestations of a rare power of purchase. There was much indeed in the tone in which Adam Verver spoke again, and who shall say where his thought stopped? "*Le compte y est.* You've got some good things."

Maggie met it afresh—"Ah, don't they look well?" [2, 368f.]

The careful reader, with "a view more penetrating than the occasion really demanded," need not be reminded that, for James, people were not to be treated as objects.[4]

At the end of the book Maggie is more convinced than ever that Adam's pasty world is the only beautiful one, and she intends to preserve it as best she can. Far from broadening that world to include Amerigo, she has simply drawn a contrite and converted Amerigo into the fold. Although Adam himself has transferred much of his power to Maggie, and in a sense is stepping out of the picture by taking Charlotte off to America, he has succeeded in his struggle to free Maggie from "worldliness." Charlotte's genuine, thwarted love for Amerigo turns her into a pathetic and rather appealing figure at the end, but the Ververs' praise of her is mere condescension. The final merging of American and European interests leaves Charlotte rather abruptly out. This is contradictory not only to the spirit of mercy which has characterized the entire second half of the book, but also to James's carefully drawn portrait of Charlotte as a partially sympathetic figure. The symbolic theme of America redeeming and revitalizing Europe, while unmistakably present, seems to be offered with a certain moral reserve on the author's part.

In spite cf this, Maggie's achievement is a moral one, and indeed a great one. She has taken the basically amoral power at her fingertips and turned it to the best advantage of which she is humanly capable. I say humanly, for there is really nothing supernatural about her sacrifice, and we cannot appreciate it properly unless we see it in its social context. James knew that power was intrinsically neither good nor bad. He saw, further, that the most colossal massing of power in his-

---

4. Here again, of course, we are dealing with a passage that admits of more than one reading. The "power of purchase" may be taken as an allusion to the religious analogy of Christ's "purchase" of mankind through His sacrifice, and Maggie's and Adam's tone may be whimsical when they appear to be gloating. But Adam's "objectification" of Charlotte and Amerigo is also the result of a tendency he has exhibited from the first—an inability to think in any but financial terms. If his businesslike manner on this occasion hides a benevolent feeling for Amerigo, it also hides a total lack of consideration for Charlotte. As ever, he thinks of them only as they may serve or endanger Maggie, not as individuals who deserve respect in themselves.

tory was taking place in American capitalism, and that although the act of gathering such power was morally deadening, the power itself might be available to noble uses—available even to a purgation of the lust after power. *The Golden Bowl* may be seen as an exploitation of the latent meaning in this situation. Adam Verver, who is capitalism almost in the abstract, bequeaths all his moral errors, his prejudices, his self-importance to Maggie; but he also gives her a consciousness of unlimited power, and hence an enormous capacity for endurance. Maggie's test arrives in a dilemma from which there is no completely satisfactory exit, and this is precisely because the dilemma is a factor of her own narrow world, hers and her father's. Charlotte and the Prince accept this world because they need its wealth, and once in it they are caught up in the childish delusions of perfection upon which Adam has based the whole structure. For them there is no way out but to appeal to Maggie, on whose behalf the delusions are maintained. Maggie's sacrifice consists in transferring the ugly truth of the adultery—the fruit of her demonstrably foolish relationship with Adam—from Amerigo's and Charlotte's shoulders to her own. Superficially nothing could seem less heroic, for Maggie is perpetuating a lie which holds her marriage together. But in reality she is being asked to deny for Amerigo's sake the whole basis of her previous belief in the goodness of her world. Adam has seen to it that she should have no suspicion of an external, evil society, but now she is suddenly faced with—and asked to continue facing—evidence not only that this society exists, but that its vices are nursed by her own power. Her own world has become a corrupt one.

It is doubtful whether Maggie ever considers that this corruption was positively invited by her father's false protectiveness, but she acts upon a further awareness which is scarcely less difficult to acknowledge. This is her recognition that however imperfect her world has now become, all of the characters are inextricably dependent on it; they *live* there. Her love for Amerigo compels her to save him at any cost. The cost is her sense of innocence. Instead of turning her face to the wall she confronts the problem of social deception directly, and masters it. Her moral awareness, we must note, grows only to the extent that she can see a "sinner," an outsider, as worthy of her best love; she never achieves the sort of inclusiveness we saw in previous heroes. But she survives a nearly total disenchantment with her most cherished assumptions, and goes on to love Amerigo so strongly that she is finally able to save him. Literally she saves him from Charlotte, and *for* herself. Symbolically she saves him from his own ignoble motives for marrying her, and enables him to keep his access to the energy of the New World. The Principino, with a mother who is power and goodness and a father who is tradition and taste, will inherit every conceivable advantage. We do not know what use he will make of them, if any; but Maggie is responsible for his freedom.

If Maggie's vision of society does not extend as far as, say, Strether's, she is nevertheless a heroine of greater stature than any of her predecessors, for she combines her spiritual love with a basic respect for the practical world of which she is a member. Milly Theale was as much a product of industrial America as Maggie is, but her power was untranslatable into action. Her lack of contact with "real life" was seen as a serious limitation in her consciousness. Maggie, however, effects a compromise between her ideals and her social duty, and hence is able to become an agent of positive good. The compromise necessarily hinders the full development of her "negative capability." She never reaches a point of intellectual and moral delicacy that we might properly call James's own. Some critics have felt that James and Maggie are equally blind in this respect, but a brief summary of James's attitudes toward his successive heroes should lead to a rather more plausible conclusion.

In *The Princess Casamassima* the hero contemplated two immediate ideals, social justice and an aristocratic cultivation of taste. Both goals attracted him, but both demanded commitments he was unprepared to make. His final attitude, which I call inclusiveness, denied the merit of a dedication to either ideal at the expense of the other. Since Hyacinth was the only genuinely inclusive figure in the book, the other characters were implicitly judged as having failed to confront reality —the sum total of human experience. In order to accept the wisdom of the hero's sacrifice we had to subordinate living to Life.

The theme of social justice was absent from *The Ambassadors,* and never became an issue again. Instead, the aristocratic or upper middle-class setting became the context of a new opposition, this time between (American) principles and (French) manners. Once again, the sensitive hero found each goal inadequate by itself—although again he seemed slightly to prefer the more sophisticated and civilized of the two.[5] As before, his eventual sense of Life was too large to be comfortably managed, and he sacrificed his comfort to a preservation of his inclusiveness. He faced an option between a compromise course and an absolutely good one, and chose the latter.

The moral issue was further clarified in *The Wings of the Dove*, where manners came into direct opposition with the philosophy of inclusiveness rather than with some lesser ideal. Since the manners in question (largely Kate Croy's) were turned to perverse ends, the victory of unmannered conscience seemed assured. Yet a curious undercurrent of dissent seemed to be accumulating. Not only was the sensitive heroine's grasp on Life brought into serious doubt, the "practical" manners of the villain were linked with a real, vital world to which the heroine herself aspired. Milly died not in heroism but in desperation; it was her previous tenaciousness to the physical world that was heroic.

Thus among other developments James was gradually emancipating himself from black-versus-white contrasts of values. It became increasingly difficult for us to make simple moral judgments about a given character, for the author took greater care to treat both sides of the question with the sympathy they deserved, and to present his drama only as it was seen by the participants. His aim was rather to increase the feeling of genuine life in his novels than to reduce his own moral awareness to that of his characters. He did not attempt to manipulate the truth and moralize about it, but rather, in his own favorite phrase, to *express* it—that is, to represent it altogether in terms of human action. Human action is not in itself moralistic. We may moralize about it, and often with good cause, but when we moralize we are dealing with it at one remove from its immediate truth. In James's later novels we can see a progressive movement toward the ideal of an action that speaks wholly for itself. Furthermore, we have seen the common basis for his situations, the International Theme, continually revised and reorganized in the interest of making his genuine moral questions more intelligible. By the time we arrive at *The Golden Bowl* James has so refined this approach that he feels free to remain completely outside of his drama.

To stay out of the drama is not merely to avoid explicit moral judg-

5. However, it should be remembered that the hero himself continued to represent a basic simplicity and austerity of mind which compensated for this new preference. Despite his attraction to Madame de Vionnet, for example, Strether never abandoned his peculiarly American type of integrity.

ments, but to eliminate the inclusive hero as well. James gradually realized that it was a form of moralizing to sift the action of his novels through the mind of a character whose eventual values were the author's own. Such heroes—the true *ficelles* in James's art, since they tell the reader just what the author expects him to think—cannot be said to exist in real life. The author of human action does not tell us what it means; *that* we must try to discover for ourselves. Although James held firm moral views, and expressed them in the ethical conflict of his characters, he refused to hamper the freedom of those characters by pushing them neatly into his moral scheme. *The Golden Bowl* ends, not on a note of moral finality which James has carefully trained one of his characters to strike, but rather on the same authentic dissonance, the perpetual clash of interests, with which the novel began. The nonsocial renunciation of worldly prejudice has been removed from the action, where it always seemed faintly improbable, and adopted by the author himself. The tragedy of manners is dissolved. If there is an inclusive hero of *The Golden Bowl,* a figure who bears the weight of a total, unspeakable knowledge, it is not Maggie but James himself. The marriage of the Old World and the New remains couched in a world of moral errors, a world which is nonetheless the only possible hope for the perpetuation of good. James's implicit criticisms of the Ververs can be found between the lines, but James himself had come to see that there was a morality beyond moralizing. His respect for Life —his love of reality in every form, however alien to his own values— becomes the force through which the characters of *The Golden Bowl* are spared a judgment day. The burden of knowledge and forgiveness is his own.